VIA Folios 87

Our Naked Lives

Essays from Gay Italian American Men

FURTHER PRAISE FOR *Our Naked Lives:*

"*Our Naked Lives* made me laugh and cry, sometimes at the same time. The essays include history, humor, religion; they are memoirs infused with poetry. These stories are poignant, timeless, and brutally honest. An enjoyable read and a welcomed addition to Italian American Studies and the LGBTQI community."
>   —Teri Ann Bengiveno, Professor of History and Women's Studies, Las Positas College

"In a community where queerness is celebrated and bonds have often been enhanced by choice of friendship rather than by birth and blood, cultural heritage has been woefully overlooked. The men of *Our Naked Lives* come out as loud and proud—of their identification as gay and Italian American. This collection of essays and reflections shows the strength and beauty of our family trees, whose stubborn roots push beyond the paved path and reach up to wave flags of their own. We'd be remiss not to take notice and pay homage, no matter our own orientation or origin."
>   —Bryan Borland, Editor of *Assaracus: A Journal of Gay Poetry*

"Editors Joseph Anthony LoGiudice and Michael Carosone have put together an extraordinary collection of essays on what it's like to grow up and live one's life proudly as Italian American and gay. The two present, through their own moving stories and the stories of the other talented men who contributed to this volume, a fascinating glimpse into the households of Italian American families. This book should be on everyone's priority reading list, including members of the LGBT community and the leaders and members of the National Italian American Foundation."
>   —Lou Chibbaro Jr., Senior News Reporter of *The Washington Blade*

"What a gift these essays are! They range widely from the most desperate moments of a gay child's life to the exhilaration of finding the courage and the community to live freely and expansively. As an Italian American woman, I found many pieces of myself in these stories, and they tell me clearly, with grace, anger, and generosity those necessary stories that nobody was supposed to know. The writers are, as Ginsberg said of Whitman, 'courage teachers.' May they be widely read!"
>   —Geraldine DeLuca, Writer and Editor of *Dialogue on Writing*, and Professor Emerita of English, Brooklyn College

"*Our Naked Lives* moved me with a sense of immediacy while harkening back to the writing of the late Robert Ferro. Reminiscences by several generations of Italian-American gay men are evocative as the memory of my Aunt Angie's calamari; yet, authors do not airbrush struggles for identity, acceptance, and love. The essays illuminate, inform, and challenge the reader and eschew stereotypes. Reflections on intersections of gender, class, and ethnicity make this collection a must-read for gender and ethnic studies courses."

> —Mark Gianino, Clinical Associate Professor, Boston University School of Social Work

"These essays do not shy away from tough topics like sexual orientation or racial prejudice in the United States. These voices can be heard throughout all of the pieces, always present, always narrating. These are accurate portrayals of what it means to be a cross-section of Italian-American and gay. You hold in your hands a book written by experts. Read it with the knowledge that you will know more today than you did yesterday."

> —Shaun Knittel, Associate Editor of *Seattle Gay News*

"The notion of what 'pride' means in the 21ˢᵗ century, and all of the challenges, complexities, and possibilities that come with our individual and collective journeys towards it have been exponentially expanded with the publication of these beautiful essays. *Our Naked Lives* reveals the rich, diverse identities and experiences of gay Italian-American men, which, until now, have remained almost entirely unknown to the rest of the world."

> —Noah Michelson, Editor of *The Huffington Post Gay Voices*

"If you are looking for a singular voice in *Our Naked Lives*, you might be disappointed. The stories feel connected, by themes of family, religion, class, and behavior, but like stories of any community, things are never simple. Contradictions abound and memories vary. For one storyteller, a stereotypical Italian male persona is an impossible model to follow; another finds comfort behind a peacock image. One writer finds some traditions smothering, while another wades through the madding crowd of holidays and family to focus on one person, as one writer tells us, a grandmother, for inspiration and humanity. This collection is like that good grandmother, who understands the value of certain traditions, while recognizing that all members of our family must be free."

> —Louis Pizzitola, author of *Hearst Over Hollywood*

"From Florida to Philly, from Rome to Bensonhurst, gay Italian-American writers share their collective experiences to find acceptance with their families and for themselves. While their journeys may differ, a common bond remains, forged from heartache and loss, defiance and love."
—Jim Provenzano, author of the Lambda Literary Award winner *Every Time I Think of You*

"This eclectic collection of 14 essays chronicles the navigation of Gay and Italian American identities. The comings out of these Gay Italian American men, in all their shapes and sizes, vividly show the urgency of challenging that long held Italian American belief in what Carosone calls 'the transformative powers of *omertà*.'"
—Paul Schindler, Editor-in-Chief of *Gay City News*

"*Our Naked Lives* is among the most moving books I have read. You don't have to be Italian American, Catholic, formerly Catholic, gay, or gay-friendly to appreciate this important gem. Soul-baring, brave, and honest, these gay Italian American men's stories will resonate with anyone who has ever felt diminished, ostracized, marginalized, humiliated, embarrassed or 'other' simply for being who he was born to be. Out of the closet and into the classroom, *Our Naked Lives* should be required reading in myriad Queer and Ethnic Studies programs. Thank you, gentlemen! You brought me tears of laughter. You brought me tears of pain. *Basta così*. May *Our Naked Lives* help bring us to a time when no one needs to cry."
—Karen Tintori, author of *Unto the Daughters: The Legacy of an Honor Killing in a Sicilian American Family*, St. Martin's Press

Our Naked Lives

Essays from Gay Italian American Men

Edited by

Joseph Anthony LoGiudice
and
Michael Carosone

BORDIGHERA PRESS

Library of Congress Control Number: 2013935891

Cover photo: *Joe Oppedisano*

Printed in the United States.

Published by
BORDIGHERA PRESS
John D. Calandra Italian American Institute
25 West 43rd Street, 17th Floor
New York, NY 10036

VIA FOLIOS 87
ISBN 978-1-59954-050-4

JOSEPH'S DEDICATIONS

To Michael: You taught me to trust myself. You taught me to empower myself. You taught me that love is more powerful than hate.

To Nanny: You are the only person in our family who is not Italian American; yet, I learned how to be proud of my identities because of your acceptance and love.

To Gay Italian American Men: You endure hate. You experience bigotry. And even when you are alienated by others, you manage to overcome these experiences and demonstrate tremendous resiliency. You are my idols.

MICHAEL'S DEDICATIONS

To Joseph, for getting me through each day; for everything; you inspire me; enough said.

To the strong, fierce women in my life—my mother, sister, grandmother, aunts, cousins, nieces, and friends—sometimes you do not realize how powerful you are.

To the writers who inspire me. To the writers who will inspire me.

To the activists who work tirelessly to make this world a better place.

To those wonderful souls who chose suicide when the world was simply too much. I respect your choices, but you must know that that was not your only choice. You are not in heaven because there is none; you live on in the memories of those whom you left behind.

ACKNOWLEDGEMENTS

We thank the founders and publishers of Bordighera Press for their acceptance of identities, voices, words, and lives: Fred Gardaphé, Paolo Giordano, and Anthony Julian Tamburri.

We thank the contributors: the remarkable Gay Italian American men who bravely shared the intimate details of their lives, in order to prove the worthiness of their existence.

We thank all of the Queer Italian American men and women, who inspired us, and continue to inspire us.

CONTENTS

INTRODUCTION

The impetus for this book derived from Michael's thesis on the marginalization of Italian American literature for his master's degree in English. While conducting his research, Michael stumbled upon two books of gay Italian American writings.[1] The only two books! At first, Michael was excited with his discovery. Then disappointment and anger erased the excitement when he realized that Gay Italian American identities and voices were not represented in literature, especially Italian American literature and Queer literature.

Immediately, Michael found copies of those two books, and that evening, he explained to Joseph his frustration about the double marginalization of Gay Italian American literature. That was the conversation that started the idea for this collection of personal essays from a diverse group of Gay Italian American men.

Joseph's response was filled with the same disappointment and anger because he, too, realized the absence of Gay Italian American identities and voices in the curriculum during his own studies in psychology and social work. However, during his undergraduate years at Columbia University, Joseph's Italian American identity was very much present when his fellow classmates typically stereotyped him as an ignorant blue-collar, working-class guido from Ben-

---

[1] *Fuori: Essays by Italian/American Lesbians and Gays*, edited by Anthony Julian Tamburri (West Lafayette, IN: Bordighera Press, 1996).
Hey Paesan!: Writing by Lesbians and Gay Men of Italian Descent, edited by Giovanna (Janet) Capone, Denise Nico Leto, and Tommi Avicolli Mecca (Oakland, CA: Three Guineas Press, 1999).

sonhurst, with his family in the mafia, who did not deserve acceptance to an Ivy League institution.

So, we talked about how both of our identities—Gay and Italian American—never appeared throughout our years of formal education. Those two characters were never written in the scenes; those two actors were never given roles on the stage. And we wondered how much longer this would continue, and how much more we were able to tolerate.

Here are two stereotypes: one, the Italian American community is perceived as ignorant, stupid, unsophisticated, uncultured, blue-collar, working-class, and connected to the mafia; two, the gay community is perceived as intelligent, sophisticated, cultured, creative, white-collar, and high class. Thus, a contradiction is formed, creating identity crises among Queer Italian American men and women.

Furthermore, in the mainstream, heterosexual society, the stereotype for the Italian American male is a man who is macho, strong, tough, brutish, violent, uneducated, handsome, sexy, and virile, with a big penis and an even bigger sex drive. Thus, commonly, Gay Italian American men distance themselves from their ethnic selves because they cannot, and do not want to, fulfill the stereotype of the Italian American male.

Contrary to the negative stereotype, Gay men can be macho; however, Gay Italian American men do not want to associate themselves with the negative stereotype of Italian American male machismo. Therefore, they denounce their ethnic halves because they do not feel comfortable in/with their own families and ethnic communities. They disconnect from their Italian American history, heritage, and culture. They give themselves fully to their homosexual selves because they are more accepted in their queer communities. However, they are only accepted as non-ethnic, white gay men, not as ethnic Italian American Gay men, who can also identify as non-white if they so choose to do so.

We have noticed a lack of ethnic pride between Gay Italian American men. Hence, gay Italian American male writers write about their gay lives, communities, culture, and history, but not about their Italian American lives, communities, culture, history, and heritage. Such an identity crisis must be solved and corrected by both communities: the Gay Community and the Italian American Community. Furthermore, such stereotypes are debilitating for, both, the individuals and the communities.

It must also be stated that such issues do not occur only in the ethnic Italian American community, but in many ethnic communities, as homosexuality is still not accepted, tolerated, and understood in many communities and societies.

Ethnicity and homosexuality can be viewed as mutually exclusive, and when the two interact, they create a conflicted relationship. And it is the conflict that must be resolved in order for a Queer Italian American to live a healthy and fulfilled life, in which he/she is proud and accepting of, both, his/her ethnicity and sexuality.

In the mainstream literary world, and in society in general, there exists levels of marginalization within one already marginalized ethnic community: first, all Italian American writers, regardless of gender, are marginalized; second, Italian American women writers are marginalized even more because of their gender; and third, queer Italian American writers are marginalized even further because of their sexual orientation.

A major, reoccurring theme in Gay Italian American literature is rejection. Queer Italian American writers—and their characters—are rejected because they refuse to conform to the traditions, mostly religious, of their families. They feel like outsiders. They are ostracized and oppressed because they are different. They become alone

3

and lonely. Ironically, in essence, they are treated the same way their immigrant ancestors were treated by the mainstream society when they arrived in America from Italy.

Although Americans of the Gay, Lesbian, Bisexual, Transgender, and Queer (GLBTQ) community and population have made great strides, their futures, at times, seem uncertain, insecure, and grim because of the heterosexist society in which they live. Their civil rights continue to be debated and threatened.

The Gay Community, to no fault of its own, is a group of which many different types of people belong, from many different walks of life. It is unique in that, unlike any other group of people, its members come from every group of people, from every race, religion, class, and culture. Usually, the only thing that homosexuals have in common is that they are attracted to the same sex. Thus, ethnicity is easily overlooked in the gay community. And lately, queer men and women are fighting for their civil rights, so their ethnic rights are not a priority.

The purpose of this book is to present these essays that inform on the experiences of these men and their lives as part of the diverse fabric of American society. The lives of these writers are complex because they are forced to conform into a society that demands that they do not express their sexual and ethnic identities, with pride, in positive ways. As sexual and ethnic minorities, these men experience double discrimination.

Many people will ask why this book is important and unique, and why this group of men is important and unique. Our answer to that often ubiquitous and trite question is this: Our identities, voices, words, and lives are important and unique because the intersection of our sexuality and ethnicity does not allow us to fit in to the mainstream American society and culture, thereby keeping us in the margins. And it should be common sense and common knowledge by now, in the twenty-first century, that no human being deserves to be marginalized for any reason.

This book has been a labor of love for us since 2008, and we hope that our readers take this journey with us, and appreciate the important lives and words of our contributors.

This Is What I Remember

Michael Carosone

I remember everything; yet, I remember nothing. I remember more bad than good. I remember more misery, pain, and suffering than happiness. I remember the loneliness and discomfort of growing up gay in a heterosexual world.

This is what I remember.

This is what I remember.

SUICIDE

I remember the constant thoughts of wanting to commit suicide. Or, more so, the constant thoughts of not wanting to exist. My attempts were pathetic and cliché: trying to swallow a lot of aspirin, holding the razor blade to my wrist, sticking my head in the oven, tying a rope to a pipe. But I was never brave enough to succeed.

SUICIDE
The blood mixes
through the streams of veins

blue lines
decorating the skin

when cut and tasted
the juice is sweet

Life is blended
through the body

and when sliced
life is drained

and the problems
are peeled away

no more pain and suffering
Death is the only way

LONELINESS

My youth was consumed with loneliness, feelings of not belong-
ing, and thinking of ways to kill myself. I experienced many dark
nights of the soul. And television saved me. Although I read a lot, I
looked to TV for the noise to comfort me, and make me feel less
lonesome. Reading is a solitary act, not always the best thing for a
lonely person. As a teenager, I was alone many Friday and Saturday
nights because my single-parent mother worked as a waitress, and
my teenage sister was either working, too, or out with her friends.
Those nights, I was at home by myself, sitting on the sofa, or lying in
bed, watching TV shows. *The Golden Girls* got me through many
lonely Saturday nights—not so much the TV show, but those four
extraordinary women. I was a gay boy, and I knew it, and I yearned
to have friends like those four elderly women.

LONELY
As I walk through the land,
I'm all alone.
There's no one holding my hand.
People can be so cold.
There's no one to hold.
I'm all alone.
No one cares,
But everyone stares.
I wish someone knew me.

Then someone would love me.
I'm all alone,
As I walk through the land.
I'm all alone,
No one to hold my hand.

IDENTITY CRISIS #1

I remember my first identity crisis. I hated being me practically my entire life. I hated being Italian American practically my entire life. I hated the negative stereotypes associated with being Italian American; I did not want to admit that I was American of Italian descent because of such negative stereotypes and images. As a young child, I wanted to change my last name to "Carson," or something else "non-Italian." I was embarrassed and ashamed of who I was and where I came from. My identity was in a crisis, and it would not be until many years later—in my adulthood—after reading much about Italian Americans, written by Italian Americans, that my identity crisis would come to an end. Literature has amazing powers that can change the lives of the readers; literature saved my life.

IDENTITY CRISIS #2

I remember my second identity crisis. Later in life, I would come to realize that my ethnicity was not the only aspect of my life that marginalized me, and made me not "fit in." As a homosexual male, my sexual orientation also marginalized me, and made me feel like an outcast, made me feel less than human. And it must be stated, and known, that with its conservative and traditional ways of thinking, the Italian American community—my own community—has not always been accepting and understanding of my sexual orientation. Ironically, one marginalized community marginalizes—even minimizes and oppresses—another marginalized community.

I remember when I was a young child in elementary school. Ironically, I cannot remember the exact age. I had a difficult time relating to the other students. I knew that I did not "fit in." I was not the only American of Italian descent, but I was one of the few in a school with mostly Jewish American and Irish American children. And of course, I befriended the other three to five children who were also Italian American. We formed a close bond.

A CHILDHOOD OF FEAR AND ANXIETY: A MEMORY

The entire week before Frank's birthday party was one of the worst and most anxious weeks of my childhood. Frank was my friend and classmate. I was nine years old, and it was the summer after we finished the fourth grade. Frank had invited all of the boys from the class to his backyard birthday pool party. I did not want to attend, but my mother forced me to go because, the previous October, Frank had come to my birthday party with one of his flashy gifts--how very "Italian American" of him.

Frank's family was known for giving ostentatious gifts. They were show-offs. But that was not why I invited Frank to my birthday parties. Actually, I never liked his gifts. I invited him because we were close friends since the first grade; we truly liked each other and each other's company; and if I remember correctly, I think that I had a crush on Frank. He was one of those tough, rugged kids, with the voice to match.

Anyway, I did not want to attend Frank's birthday party because of football. Yes, football! It was known for a while that we would play football at the party. Football was the main event on the itinerary. I did not give this scary thought much attention until the week before the party. It was then that the fear and anxiety crept in. No, not crept in. Barreled in. I hated football. I hated all sports. I did not know how to play football, and I would be forced to do so. I was the stereotypical gay boy. And if I did not necessarily know that I was gay, I knew that I was different. And one of my many differences was that I hated football. However, I needed to keep this hatred a secret for fear that the other boys would think that I was weird, and not a real boy—a sissy, as I was called in the past.

ETHNICITY

I am third-generation Italian American, which probably makes me more American than Italian. And I know for a fact that my "Americanization" (whatever that ubiquitous coined term really means) has made me lose my "Italianness," which is not a positive or a negative; it simply is what happened, and what happens. Honestly, I do not mind that I am more American than Italian; after all, I was born and live in the United States, and should have some pride in where I was born, and where I live, as should all people. Actually, more ethnic groups living in America need to embrace the fact that they are as much American as they are from their other ethnicities. That notwithstanding, I am only able to be a patriotic American because of my questioning of and disagreement with the American government, citizenry, and society in general—a true patriotic American does this; sadly, most Americans do not. I am also able to be a proud American because I am able to look at the United States through an objective lens, with the eyes of a queer person who still has not been granted his full civil rights.

Nevertheless, I simply do not want to neglect the fact that my family came from Italy, and that there will always be a part of me *from* that country and culture, and *in* that country and culture until the day I die. However, the mainstream American society has been instrumental in hammering away my Italian heritage. Throughout American history, Italian immigrants and Italian Americans have been required to blend into the American culture, thus surrendering their own identities, and relinquishing their origins.

ANCESTRY

I remember hearing the stories of my ancestry. My maternal grandparents were born in the United States. For better lives and futures, their parents (my great-grandparents) immigrated to America from an impoverished village in Napoli (Naples), southern Italy. Their story is a common and typical Italian immigrant tale. They lived next door to each other on Dean Street, in Brooklyn, New York—a working-class, blue-collar neighborhood, which was heavily populated with Italian immigrants. They fell in love and were married at a young age. They were more connected to their Italian heritage than I. However, they, too, were forced to surrender their "Italianness."

As for my paternal ancestry, I do not know much about them. My father abandoned my mother, my sister (when she was four years old), and me, when I was eighteen months. My mother never talked about him much, and her sister (my aunt) kept one photograph—the *only* photograph—of him. I only know my father from that one photograph, and a few stories that my aunt told me. He was of Sicilian descent, born in the United States. He was a Vietnam War veteran, which was probably the cause of his drug addiction and psychological ailments.

CRYING SINCE BIRTH: A MEMORY

Either I do not remember the whole story, or the entire story was never told to me. I only know about my father from the few fragmented stories that were told to me: the bits and pieces of a complex puzzle that I will never be able to put together. This is what I remember: I was an infant with colic, who constantly cried. What great irony and foreshadowing this was. Maybe my tears did not come from my stomach pains, but from my soul's pain. I was told that my father put a gun to my head because he could no longer tolerate my crying. Or, tolerate me. I was also told that he never wanted me, never wanted a second child. During those dark nights of the soul when I was a lonely child, thinking about killing myself, I always wished that my father would have pulled that trigger and ended my misery.

DARK, TRUTHFUL WISHES
I wish for dead
where I can lay my head
in everlasting rest
to make my life the best.
I wish for disease
in order to ease
the burden of real
life. I don't want to feel.
I wish for attention,
not to mention
love and compassion and care.
Oh, please won't they dare!

MY PARENTS

I remember hearing some other stories about my father. My mother filed for a divorce in 1976, after discovering that he was committing adultery. My father's traditional Italian American way of thinking forced my mother to quit her job once they married: "no wife of his would work." He demanded that she stay home to care for him, his future children, and his apartment. It was the mid-1970s, and I guess the Women's Liberation Movement did not fully reach my mother, who was also somewhat traditional in her Italian American way of thinking.

After the separation and divorce, my mother was left alone with two young children. It was difficult for her to work full-time while raising two toddlers, so she applied for, and received, public assistance. This was also difficult for her to accept because the traditional Italian American in her did not believe in taking any "handouts," but, rather, believed in working for, and earning, a living. My mother was forced to swallow her pride, and to enter the sometimes humiliating world of public assistance. She did not have many choices because she only had a high school diploma. At that time, more and more jobs and careers were requiring college degrees. She had two children to raise. And at that time, resources for working mothers, such as day-care and after-school programs were uncommon and limited. Ironically, the job my mother had at the telephone company, before she married my father, was secure and progressive.

So, while raising her two children, receiving public assistance, and working part-time, my mother entered community college, and earned an Associate's Degree, a major accomplishment, which would lead to a career and detachment from public assistance. Once again, her Italian American pride shined when she became self-sufficient and independent, which she truly was from the day she was born, until she was suppressed by my father, who was the wrong choice of a husband. From my mother *and* my Italian American ancestry, I was taught, and learned, how to survive and how to be resilient. Such survival skills and resiliency came in handy throughout the many years of my wanting to give up and end my life. Nothing but hope got me through.

MY NAME

I remember this about my name. My father wanted to name me Victor, after himself. But my mother won, and named me Michael, after her father. But my grandfather never thought that that was good enough because my last name was not his last name. Or, maybe I was not good enough. So, I was not completely named after him. Years later, my mother's brother—my grandfather's son—had a son, and named him after my grandfather. This new baby would have my grandfather's first and last names. This time, the naming was complete. This time, the naming was good enough. This time, the naming was perfect.

(Un)Happy Holidays: A Memory

It was Christmas Eve, 1989, I was in the eighth grade, and I was explaining to my family the latest trends in fashion, what was "cool" and "uncool" for eighth graders to wear. I was telling them about the popular fragrances. My grandfather turned to me and said: "What perfume do you wear?" That was the moment when I knew that I was truly "different," and that "different" was not good, and that I would live the rest of my life as "different," constantly explaining and defending my "differences." If my own family could not accept my "differences," then how could the rest of society?

Coming Out of the Dark Gay Closet

I remember that when I came out of the dark gay closet, my family told me that they always knew, and that they still loved and accepted me. Although painful enough, with years of pain and misery behind it, my coming out was not as painful as others'. However, I wondered and asked my family, why, if they knew that I was gay from a young age, did they not discuss it with me and help me with the process of coming out. They said that they wanted me to come out when I was ready. And I wondered whether or not they knew about my "difference" back on that Christmas Eve night in 1989 when my grandfather, who obviously knew that I was gay, looked at me with scorn in his eyes and disappointment on his face, for I would never be the grandson that he hoped for and expected me to be. And I wondered about the significance of waiting until after my grandfather's death to come out to my family. And still, I wonder why something as basic and natural as sexuality continues to divide families, destroy relationships, cause so much pain and suffering, hatred and violence, and make so many people so very afraid.

THIS IS WHAT I KNEW

At a very young age, I knew that I was different, but maybe I did not know that I was gay. Maybe I did not know what gay was. Or, maybe I knew exactly what gay was, but was too ashamed and frightened to admit that I was gay. Of course, as I grew older, I knew exactly what my difference was, and I learned, very quickly, exactly how to survive with my difference. Although I preferred death over life, I knew how to survive as a gay male in a very straight world.

This is what I remember.

This is what I remember.

ITALIAN AMERICAN PRIDE

I remember the first time that I was proud to be Italian American. It all started at a film festival in New York City—Manhattan to be exact, during September of 1997. It was then and there that I wanted to re-associate myself with my ancestry, heritage, and culture. (Later on, in October of 2001, I would become the recipient of the National Italian American Foundation's Italian American Youth Award in the Arts and Education because of my success with the second film festival, and my devotion to educating the public on Italian American issues.)

It must be stated that the film festival had special showcases of films from filmmakers of (what it considered to be) "marginalized groups": African/Black American, Asian American, and Hispanic/Latino American. However, Italian Americans were never acknowledged as a marginalized group by the organizers of the film festival, the same way that they are not recognized as a marginalized group by American society in general. It is this gross distortion that has constantly allowed for Italian Americans to be ignored as a minority group within the larger context of American society. It must be understood and accepted that Italian-Americans are marginalized in everyday life of American society, and that they deserve the same recognition, benefits, and praise as other marginalized groups. They can no longer be disregarded.

It must also be stated that the flawless and successful assimilation of the Italian immigrants into mainstream American culture has been as harmful as it as been beneficial: the disappearance of their ethnic and cultural identities, and the prosperity of their new lives and futures. Italian Americans have managed to morph into all aspects of American society, whether personal or professional, conforming to the status quo. They have become successful people.

Nevertheless, I was the facility manager of the theatre in which the films were screened. It was there that I met an eccentric and inspiring woman, one of my volunteers, who was offering her time because of her love for the art of film. We bonded immediately (maybe because of our shared ethnicity), and would become friends, and she would change my life for the better. She was older than I (I was 21 years old; she was in her mid-forties), with an abundance of wisdom and invaluable advice. More importantly, she was Italian American (or American of Italian descent), and she encouraged me to embrace my ancestry, heritage, and culture. She would make it possible for me to accept and be proud of my "Italianness and "Italian Americanness" (yes, there is a difference). She awakened my "Italianness" as much as my "Americanness."

She was born in the United States to parents who emigrated from Sicily, like the other millions of Italian immigrants during the early part of the 20th century. And like all other Italian immigrants in the United States, they were forced, and forced themselves, to assimilate into the American society and culture. They were in search of "better" lives, and did whatever it took to obtain such.

She was raised as an Italian American, speaking Italian and English, learning both cultures, understanding her heritage, appreciating the opportunities that the "New World" had to offer. She was not ashamed of her parents and Italian culture and heritage; her parents taught her to welcome it, to be grateful for it, and to love it. Unlike me, she did not experience the self-loathing. She was proud and happy to be a first generation American of Italian descent. She was comfortable with being Italian American.

She taught me much about Italian American history and culture, and about myself. She encouraged me to admire, respect, and enjoy my ethnicity and myself. Because of her, I knocked down the walls of self-loathing, which I had built so very high and strong over many years, in order to accept and appreciate my lineage. Pardon the cliché, but I returned to roots. I realized that I had to learn more about who I was, where I came from, and where I wanted to be.

After the film festival closed, we opened our minds to the prospects of organizing our own film festival devoted to Italian-American films, filmmakers, issues, themes, and culture. But after thinking about creating a film festival with such a narrow focus, I decided to start a film festival in Brooklyn, New York, as an artistic and cultural event for the local people of the borough, focusing on more than one ethnic group. Due to the marginalization of Italian American filmmakers and films in the United States (with the exception of a few), I was worried that a film festival screening only Italian American films, by Italian American filmmakers, covering Italian

American issues and culture, would not find an audience. I was worried that no one would care enough to attend; or, that people would only attend if the stereotypical "mafia/mobster/gangster films" were screened. I refused to show that film genre; I refused to intensify and promote the marginalization of Italian American filmmakers and films. And I refused to screen any films portraying Italian Americans in a negative light. Therefore, I decided to dedicate one showcase of film screenings to Italian American filmmakers and their stories, their voices, their films, and their works of art.

The film festival as a whole was a success, receiving attention from influential people of the film industry. More importantly, the Italian American filmmakers' showcase was a success, and it brought much needed and deserved attention to the Italian American filmmakers and the struggles they face, as a marginalized group, in bringing their films—their stories, voices, perspectives, art—to the mainstream audiences.

VOICE, PART ONE: A POEM

I have found my voice
my Italian American voice

it was lost for too long
but I found it
underneath all of the neglect and negativity
I have found it

it is not red or white or green

and it is not
sweetened with vino
not drenched with olive oil
not seasoned with basil
oregano
not served with tomatoes

no food
period

it is angry

it will not be contained in your convenient stereotype

it demands respect
attention
to be heard

no more oppression
no more silence (no more omertà)

it wants to sing
but not opera

it doesn't mind not fitting in
it doesn't mind being the outcast
it doesn't mind being different
unique

non-conformist

it doesn't want to play the world's absurd games

but it wants a seat at the table
not the dinner table
it wants to be noticed
valued
honored
praised

above all
it simply wants to be heard

Listen!

GAY PRIDE

I can't remember. No, wait. I felt it when I watched my first New
York City Gay Pride March (Parade) colorfully strolling down Fifth
Avenue. Yes, I was very proud to be gay.

It's still a work in progress.

But, it's getting better.

VOICE, PART TWO: A POEM[2]

I have found my voice
my gay voice

it was lost for too long
but I have found it

it was hated, hushed, and harassed
hiding, held hostage
frightened and fading
oppressed and orphaned—abandoned
bullied and beaten
ignored and isolated
tortured and tormented
drowned and dying

but now it screams

LOUD

It is angry. It is vengeful.
and it is not a rainbow
not lavender, not pink
not a triangle

---

[2] First published in *Gay City: Volume One*, edited by Vincent Kovar, Gay City
Health Project, 2008.

it is what it is
it is its own—no more apologies

and it does not have a lisp
and it does not swish
it does not sing show tunes
it does not decorate
nor does it do hair
but it can if it wishes

it will not be contained in your convenient stereotype

it is not a sinner
nor is it a saint
it doesn't believe in that religious nonsense anyway
it is not deviant/abnormal
it is not evil

it will not conform—it likes that it does not have to

it will not straighten its bend for you
it will straighten nothing for you
period

gaily, it screams
it screams it's gay

Listen. It demands to be heard.

WALKING OUT OF THE DARKNESS

I remember when I participated in the Out of the Darkness Walk for the American Foundation for Suicide Prevention. The heterosexuals were surprised when they were informed by the organizers that suicide is highest in gay youth. "Wow, they haven't a clue," I thought. The fact is that many gay people have contemplated suicide. And why is this a surprise? Most gay people are told by their families and communities that they are abnormal, disgusting, worthless, sick, and sinful. So, after a while one cannot help to believe what one has heard, what one has been taught, what one has been brainwashed to think and believe. And for those gay people who overcome such hatred, and do not believe the lies, they have difficulty with their self-esteem and self-worth. Believe me, I know.

A DIFFERENT KIND OF ESCAPE
pills
a knife
rope
a razor
some gas
and poison
the house
an oven
a ceiling fan
a pillow
a car
and garage
the house
bottles
containers
and jars
a kitchen
drawer
the house
but he
leaves
in a
different
way

red
river
flowed
ran
rolled
spilled
moved
and
spread
throughout
the house

SUICIDE IN THE CLASSROOM

I remember reading Sylvia Plath's poems and Dorothy Parker's "Resume" to my students while teaching my lessons on poetry and instructing them on how to analyze each word, each line. They thought that the poems were depressing. I thought: "If only they read my poems; now, that's depressing." And I always thought Parker's poem to be exhilarating and saving because the speaker wants to live and she wants all of us to live, too. But maybe my students thought it depressing because they never slept in the swamp of suicide, never played in the pit of pain, never danced in the dungeon of despair, and were never condemned to the cave of cruelty.

As I read the poems, tears collected in my eyes and blurred my vision. My Aunt Lisa always told me to have a good cry, that the tears wash away the suffering—let it all out, let out the pain. My problem was that I never wiped away the tears, and they would absorb in my skin, so the pain never went way.

MEMORIES OF OTHER GAY ITALIAN AMERICAN MEN

At the age of 31, my ex-boyfriend's homosexuality was still not accepted by his Italian American family members. Since he was a teenager, he was out of the closet; yet, his family did not want to acknowledge and talk about his homosexuality. They believed in the transformative powers of silence—or *omerta*—and if they did not discuss his homosexuality, then it did not exist, or it could change, or it could be cured. They held on to the communicative traditions and superstitions of their southern Italian immigrant ancestors. They continued to believe that he would one day marry a woman, settle down, and have a family, with a house, a secure job, and a pension plan—more traditional thinking. They knew that we were a couple, but.... Ironically, it did not matter that we were in a long-term relationship, living together as registered domestic partners. His mother and grandmother labeled and considered me his "friend." Well, "friends" do not have intimate, romantic, sexual relationships! Our relationship was simply too difficult for his father to handle, so we never met.

An out gay Italian American male friend of mine was in a relationship with a closeted gay Italian American man, who was married to a woman, had two children, and was a police officer. He was unable to come out of the closet because his family would not have accepted his homosexuality, so he divided his time between his two lives: married, straight, macho police officer with children; and partnered, "straight-acting," gay man, who was not accepting of his own identity and sexuality. He allowed his family to control his life, and dictate to him normal and tolerable behavior.

Yes, many gay Italian American men disgrace their families. And no, many gay Italian American men do not disgrace their families. It is all relative, and it depends on the family. I have observed both sides of the paradox. I have known both: gay Italian American men who have been accepted by their families when they came out of the closet; and gay Italian American men who have been rejected by their families, making them wish that they had remained in the closet. So, a very important question to ask is: Why must sexuality be repressed for ethnicity; or, ethnicity for sexuality? Why must we repress one for the other? The answer to such a question lies in the strict gender codes of every ethnicity, religion, and society. And the queer community must continue to ask why the straight community believes heterosexual love to be better than homosexual love.

COMING OUT OF ANOTHER CLOSET

Years ago, I removed the hinges from the door of the religious closet and came out as an Atheist. My mother responded better to my coming out as gay. To this day, she still does not believe that I am an Atheist, and tells me that even if I don't believe in organized religion, I must believe in God. Whatever she believes is fine with me. But what she does not understand is that I refuse to believe in something that has caused me such pain throughout my life. And I refuse to be a part of something that does not want me as I am.

In those two closets, I left the status quo a long time ago. I refused to conform to the ideals of others. I refused to join the absurdity and hypocrisy.

VOICE, PART THREE: A POEM
I have found my voice
My atheist voice

Oh, God, how it was lost

Lost because it is the only thing rational
in a very irrational world
Lost because it is the only thing logical
in a very illogical society

Lost because it is the only thing fearless
in a very fearful family

Lost like Moses and Jesus and Mohammad and Buddha and Krishna

The last closet door flung open
and my atheist voice came out, flew out
like the angels flying up to Heaven

My atheist voice was ignored, silenced, berated
No one wanted to hear from it and talk about it
It is a miracle that it has survived

Its bible is a book of philosophy
Not a book of myths and fairy tales

A book of literary fiction
Not a book of secrets and lies

A book of poetry
Not a book of psalms and hymns

Its gospel is freedom and independence and intelligence
Not oppression and brainwashing and ignorance

My atheist voice
believes in love and peace and nonviolence
Not hatred and war and murder
It does not follow the ideals of those religions

Listen

THIS IS WHAT I KNOW AND WILL ALWAYS REMEMBER
    William Faulkner wrote: "Some things you must always be unable to bear—injustice and outrage and dishonor and shame—just refuse to bear them." I can no longer bear being rejected, marginalized, ignored, silenced, and invisible. No one should have to. And

as a gay Italian American man I don't want to. Whether in my ethnic community or my gay community. And in society in general.

Unless the Italian American community acknowledges and accepts its gay members, and unless the gay community acknowledges and accepts its Italian American ethnic members, nothing will change for the better, and queer Italian Americans will continue to lose pieces of their identities by denouncing parts of their identities.

I think that it is time that we do some self-analysis, and ask ourselves why we are the way we are and what needs to change. We need to change the ways in which we categorize, label, and divide ourselves for the benefit of a few and for the misery of many. We need to change our languages, symbols, and signs so that all people are accepted. The best ingredient for a recipe of change is hope. We need to be hopeful that the world will change for the better—even though, at times, change seems impossible. In following with Gandhi's words, I want to be the change that I want to see. I hope that my work is meaningful, informing and enhancing society, and effecting positive change for the lives of those who are members of ethnic and sexual minority groups, bringing them from the margins to the center.

THIS IS WHAT I REMEMBER

So, you asked me what I remember. This is what I remember. Why do you ask? What exactly do you want to know? What do *you* want me to remember?

You asked me what I remember. Maybe the better question should be: What do you want to forget? I have wanted to forget so much, but unfortunately, I am unable to do so. It is as important to forget as it is to remember.

Remember this.

This is what I want *you* to remember.

A BETTER ENDING

It would be a lie if I said that I no longer think about suicide. But the truth is that those thoughts are not as frequent as they once were. It is still a cruel world, and sometimes I think about escaping it. But then I realize that it is better to live in this cruel world, with the people and things that I love, than to escape without them. It is impossible to separate the bad from the good, the same way that it is impossible to detach my sexual identity from my ethnic identity. So, I survive, and I live, and I hope, and I hope, and I hope.

VAGUELY, THE END
I have chosen not to go through with it.
I haven't done it.
I haven't succeeded,
But maybe succeeded in other ways.
I will live.
The End.

MORE ITALIAN AMERICAN THAN CATHOLIC: COMING OUT TO MY PARENTS, 1974

John D'Emilio

Gay Liberation insisted that we come out. We were all to come out, all the time, to everyone. We had to come out at work and in school, to our friends and to our families, where we worshipped and where we played. We had to come out on buses and subways, in movie houses and restaurants, on the streets and in parks and at the beach. Wherever we gathered and they gathered, too, we were to come out. Wherever heterosexuals displayed their orientation, which was pretty much everywhere, we displayed ours.

We deluded ourselves that we were following the Gay Lib script, but it didn't always work out that way. An unintended effect of Gay Liberation's message was to make many of us so angry at heterosexuals—angry at the ease with which they showed their selves, angry at what they had done to us, angry at how little they seemed even to notice their privilege and our oppression—that, no sooner had we come out than we withdrew from any substantial contact with as many of them as possible. Lesbians at least gave this a name; they called it separatism. Gay men simply surrounded themselves with other gay men.

Still, good Catholic boy that I was, I tried to follow the new doctrine. Carlos and I walked down the streets of Manhattan with our arms around each other. We sat on the grass in Central Park and smooched, like other couples were doing. We held hands at the movies. When we were out together and about to head in different directions, one of us pecked the other on the cheek. In graduate school, I felt no hesitation in inviting my peers over to my apartment, where the presence of Carlos and a king-sized bed visible from the living room, spoke volumes. I talked about Carlos the same way that my schoolmates spoke of their girlfriends and boyfriends and husbands and wives. When I got involved in the creation of what became the Gay Academic Union, I talked about that, too.

Even with all this, coming out to my Italian Catholic parents was beyond imagining. Over the years, there had been too many bruising fights. We fought over curfew. We fought over where I had just spent an evening, and with whom. We battled over whether I would go to Fordham or Columbia, whether I'd live at home or in the dorms, whether I'd stay in the dorms or move off campus and, later, over whether I'd return home to the Bronx after graduation or remain in Manhattan. We fought about Vietnam and about the draft and about every antiwar demonstration they saw on the evening news. We fought over the student strike at Columbia and we fought over my decision to boycott graduation even though they had paid through their teeth for my four years of college. We fought about going to Mass on Sunday. We even fought over Richard Nixon. Nothing was easy between us.

Although Dad could lose it now and then, Mom generally led the charge in these battles. Sometimes, in the middle of one of our explosions, the thought would cross my mind that it had been like this once for her, too. She had watched each of her older sisters—Anna and Lucy and Jenny—butt heads with Grandpa over one thing or another: who wanted to wear make-up and who wanted to stay in high school and who wanted to date the wrong boy. Her sisters had lost these fights and so had she, and all she knew how to do now was to pass down to her son a legacy of laying down the law and refusing to budge. But this thought was too inconvenient to allow it to linger. I had no room for empathy. I was in there fighting, intent on winning.

Things got simpler after graduation. I was officially an adult now. I wasn't living under their roof, and I was supporting myself, however meagerly. It was like the armistice after a long war of independence: cordiality and the restoration of diplomatic relations, but no deep connections. Conversations stopped being real. I listened to what they had to say about this family member or that one, about what was happening in Parkchester or at Berkey Photo, and I responded. We still watched baseball games on Sundays, in the summer, when I was home for a meal. But I told them as little as possible about my life. What would I have talked about? My latest acid trip? The radical history I was reading every week in graduate school? The struggle with Carlos to open up our relationship and have sex with others? I don't think so.

The fact is that, when it came to being gay, I had become a practiced liar of the first rank. I knew how to cover over by silence, or fill with invention, the time and space taken up by my secret gay life. It hadn't been hard to do. It always amazed me when, as a teenager, I arrived home after just having sex, and my whole body was still jangling with terror. My soul was shamed and waves of remorse were crashing over me. I'd drop my book bag in the living room and start yapping about my day at Regis as if nothing of any consequence had happened. Mom and dad didn't seem to notice a thing. Later, when they did start to sense something, resulting in God-awful fights with them, shouting "where have you been?" and "what have you been doing?," I still managed never to reveal a thing, even when out-yelling them.

If I had just been content to have a gay life, I'd never have needed to come out to them. After all, isn't that what the closet had meant for the generation before me? For decades, gay men had run all over New York having the time of their lives, while carefully masking it from everyone they knew who wasn't queer. Even as a gay activist, I might have preserved Mom's and Dad's ignorance, and my silence. What was the likelihood they would ever learn about me and the Gay Academic Union? Would they ever know if I spoke at a gay conference? I could demonstrate, I could write for a gay news rag, I could even—as I did for several months—do a news report on one of the gay radio broadcasts in town, knowing that the chance of it touching their world was pretty close to zero.

But deciding to write a dissertation on a gay history topic? As practiced in evasion as I was, this was a whole other matter. What would I do? Make up another dissertation that I talked about when I saw them? And when I finished and they asked to see it? No, doing the dissertation meant that the final coming out, like Judgment Day, was at hand.

The habit of avoidance dies hard. I couldn't grasp how I would arrive in the Bronx for dinner one evening, sit them down, and say "there's something I need to talk to you about." What then? Blurt out that I'm gay? This was 1974. Would they even know what that meant? Tell them I'm a homosexual? I'd have lost them after the second syllable. So, I planned to get them there slowly, to prepare them conversation by conversation until the moment of the final revelation.

A couple of months after I had passed my exams, I came home for Sunday afternoon dinner, as I did every two or three weeks. We had finished eating, and Jimmy had gone to his room to finish some homework. I looked up from my cup of coffee and said, "Well, I don't have a specific topic yet for my dissertation, but I think I've at least settled on the general area that I'll work in."

"Oh, what is it?" Dad asked.

"I think I'm going to write about some aspect of the history of sex."

Mom was sitting right across the table from me. A look of immense distaste swept across her face, as if she had just swallowed something foul. "Oh ... no ... John," she said, "not SEX!" The final word spoken with great emphasis.

Meanwhile, at the same moment, from the corner of my right eye, I saw an expression of fascination cross Dad's face as he said: "Sex? Really? You can write about sex? Huh. Who ever heard of such a thing?"

Immediately, I started chattering away. "Oh, yes, of course. Historians write about everything these days. They write about streetcars and epidemics and taverns and all sorts of things that they didn't write about when you were in school. This will be great. It's a whole new field. Almost no one has done any work in it."

A couple of months later, I was back for another dinner and ready for the second installment. "Well, I still haven't settled on my exact topic yet, but I'm pretty sure I've narrowed it down to three possibilities."

"What are they?" Mom said, and I could hear the caution in her question.

"I think it'll be either prostitution or venereal disease or homosexuality."

This time they responded as one, no division of opinion between them. With perfect timing, as if they'd rehearsed their dialogue, they said in unison: "Oh ... no ... John.... Not HOMOSEXUALITY!"

I retreated very, very quickly. "Well, we'll see where things go," I told them, and shifted the conversation. Coming out was a good idea in theory, but I still wasn't ready for what I thought would be their response.

A few months later, I waded in again. "Well, I've got my topic. I'm going to research and write about where today's Gay Liberation Movement came from, what led up to it, stuff like that."

Mom looked over at me, got up from the table, and walked into the kitchen to start cleaning up after the meal. But Dad pressed me.

"Where will you find those people?" Dad asked, and he looked at me as if the answer would tell him something he didn't want to hear.

"Well that's easy. They publish magazines, and they have offices in various cities. Once I find the first few, each one will point me to others. It'll snowball. I don't think it'll be a problem."

"But why would people like that want to talk with you?" he asked.

This was my chance, I knew. I could have told him that I was one of those people, that they'd easily open up to one of their own. We would have been off and running. But I couldn't. I couldn't face their reaction; I couldn't face the fight that I knew we'd have. I wasn't up for the fury that I felt sure my announcement would spark in each one of us. I wanted to go back to dinner, finish the rest of our pastries and coffee, and return to conversations about the Giants' chances for the National League Pennant.

"Oh they're eager to talk," I started chattering. "No one pays any attention to them. They've never been written about, and this is a chance for them to tell their story and have it become a part of history. They'll talk. This will be so much easier than looking for materials from generations ago. My adviser thinks this is a great idea."

This was going to be even harder than I imagined, I realized on the subway ride home. I had taken us to the brink. I'd created the opportunity. I'd set up the situation. Dad's question gave me just the chance I'd wanted. But I pulled us back from the edge. If I sidestepped these coming out opportunities much longer, the dissertation would get absorbed into the pile of bland non-conversations we always had. "How's the dissertation going," they'd ask when I came home, and I would say, "oh fine" and soon we'd be talking about Cousin Vivian or Uncle Phil or the new priest at St. Raymond's or the new businesses on Westchester Square.

For the rest of the summer, I let the whole thing lie. I had been hired to teach part-time at Stevens Institute of Technology in Hoboken, New Jersey, and the intensity of preparation for my first semester of teaching pushed the dissertation—and almost everything else—to the back of my consciousness. In September, Mom and Dad took a long trip to the West Coast, making it even easier to delay our day of truth telling. They were delivering Jimmy to his first semester at Reed College, in Portland; stopping in San Francisco, which they'd never seen before; and then heading down south so that Mom could visit with Lucy and Anna, whom she hadn't seen since they moved out west.

While they were gone, I received a call from Montclair State College. Marty Duberman had recommended me to them as someone who could teach a gay studies course in the spring. This was like a dream. We talked about this all the time in the Gay Academic Union (GAU), and here and there someone, usually a senior faculty member, had the guts to do it. It was thrilling and terrifying at the same time, a validation of the choices I was making. And a challenge: Put up or shut up. Deliver in the classroom or ... well, there was no alternative.

Mom called when they got back from the West Coast and reported on the trip, "The campus is so beautiful," she told me. "Jimmy's roommate seems to be a very nice boy." She gave me updates on all the family and the highlights of their stay in San Francisco: the cable cars and the hills and the Golden Gate Bridge.

"How are you?" she asked. "How are your classes going? You're not being mean to your students, are you?"

"They're fine. It's a lot of work. I seem to be working all the time preparing for it. I didn't know it would be so much work."

"You take after your father. He's never liked work, you know. Grandpa worked all the time."

"Yeah, Ma, I know. Listen, something great happened while you were gone. I got called about another part-time teaching job."

"Oh, really?"

"Yes, at Montclair State College, which is also in Jersey. I can take a bus from the George Washington Bridge terminal, and it will drop me off right at the entrance to the campus. They want me to teach a brand new gay studies course."

I could almost hear her teeth clench and see her jaw tightening. She always did this when she was caught off guard by something she didn't like, as if she was shutting the gate to her vocal chords so that unwanted words could not pour out.

"Why would they call *you* to teach something like *that?*"

Like a bad habit I was helpless to break, I again deflected us away from the question she wanted to ask and started jabbering. "Oh, well, you know there aren't too many people who know anything about this at all, and now that I'm working on this dissertation the word is getting around that I can do this sort of thing. It'll be a very good experience, teaching at a public university to go alongside the job at Stevens. Listen, by the way, I was thinking I'd come home for dinner at the end of the week. Is that okay?"

Traveling up to the Bronx that Friday afternoon, I was reading one of the spate of books that had come out in the early seventies, a part of that first Gay Liberation publishing wave. George Weinberg was a maverick psychologist who had broken with the professional wisdom about homosexuality as illness. He had written a small book, *Society and the Healthy Homosexual,* meant for lay readers, and aimed at heterosexuals as much as homosexuals. He had a chapter on parents and their gay children, something of a "how to" come out to them, and how parents should respond to the news. It was kind, soothing, and calm in its approach, emphasizing what a gift it was for a child to speak so honestly, and advising the gay son or daughter to recognize how hard this might be for parents to hear, and to prepare accordingly. I wasn't sure about the gift part, but I already knew that "hard" was an understatement.

Mom was all tan from her time in southern California. We talked about this and that, and she ooo-ed and aah-ed about the palm trees and the mountains and the waves along the beach. Lucy and Phil had a very nice house with an apricot and a plum and a lemon tree in their backyard. "You should see the size of those lemons," she told me. "As big as oranges."

When it was time to start preparing dinner she moved into the kitchen. She continued to tell stories about the trip, and I pulled up a chair by the kitchen door and listened to her talk, just as I had so many times when I was a child. My mind was half on what she was saying, half on the coming out story that I still couldn't quite imagine ever getting told. Pausing for a few seconds, she looked up from the cutting board where she was slicing potatoes and, waving the large knife she had in her hand, said: "John, your father and I have been talking. There's something we have to ask you and I want you to tell me the truth. Are you a gay person?"

I couldn't believe it. She was asking. Direct. No beating around the bush. This was it. My mouth involuntarily opened into a huge grin that stretched from ear to ear and I heard myself saying, "Yes, Mom, I am."

That was it. I'd done it. It was over. She asked me! Oh my God, I was thinking, everything will be different now. It's like a new beginning. I'll be able to talk to my family about something real. This is what the Second Coming must mean. Everything is good, everyone is truthful, there's warmth and love and.... And then, in the middle of these thoughts, racing so fast that I couldn't hold on to them, I noticed that my mother had gone back to slicing potatoes, and was chattering away about California and how beautiful it was, and how Anna loved taking care of her grandchildren, and how much fun the cable cars were in San Francisco. It was as if she hadn't asked and I hadn't told, as if I'd hallucinated the whole thing on an LSD trip.

I sat there in disbelief, barely hearing what she was saying, occasionally forcing out an "uh huh" and a "really?" to mask my confusion. I wandered into the living room and turned on the TV, allowing myself to get lost in the evening news. Dad got home from work and went through his usual routine. A perfunctory hello, his coat hung in the front closet, a retreat to the bedroom where he changed his clothes, and then his nightly collecting of the day's trash that he carried out to the incinerator. Meanwhile, nothing more came from Mom.

At dinner, I heard Dad's version of the vacation stories and the visit to Reed. I had resigned myself to another failed coming out attempt when I saw him put his knife and fork down and look directly at me. "John, your mother and I have been talking," I heard him start saying, "There's something we have to ask you and I want you to tell us the truth. Are you a gay person?"

"Yes, Dad, I am," I said, just as I had a couple of hours before.

The color drained from his face, and he started jerking his head rapidly from side to side. "No, no, no," he repeated. "That can't be true. It can't be. You can't be gay."

I'm thinking, "Oh my God, he's going to die. I've killed my father." Just four years ago his brother Doc had keeled over at the dinner table with no warning, dead before the ambulance arrived. Would both brothers go the same way? I started to rise from my chair and reach across the table to take his hand, when from my left I heard my mother explode "You bet he's gay! He told me the same damned thing a couple of hours ago!"

Now we were off and running. The rest of the evening is a bit of a blur, but I do remember that, for the next several hours, we talked and talked and talked. They grilled me about everything, asking about this event and that one. Was it that terrible time with Sister Perpetua in the first grade, they wanted to know. Did she drive me away from little girls? Had they been too strict with me? Should they have let me date girls sooner? "It was Regis," my mother said with definitive force after I'd brushed off several of their other explanations. "It was that all-boy's school!"

I wasn't known for my patience in encounters like this one with my parents, but I kept reminding myself "they're the ones whose lives have just changed. They're the ones who have gotten the news. They're the ones who are shocked and upset. Let this be about them, not me."

At one point my Dad said puzzlingly, "but John, I don't understand. You wanted to be a priest. You almost went into the seminary after high school."

"I know, Dad. But why do you think I backed out at the last minute? I knew I couldn't do it when I felt like this. I knew it would be impossible to deal with these attractions in the seminary."

"But, John, what about all those girls you dated, Julie and Eileen and Cathy? You went out with Eileen for a year. Were you just pretending?"

"No, Dad. I really liked them. Just because you're gay doesn't mean you never date girls."

"What about Mary Ann? You were completely infatuated with her. Your mother and I thought she was going to be the one. You had to travel over an hour to get to her house, and you'd get home so late from your dates. I know you liked her."

"I did. I really did. But it's not the same as when I'm with a guy. I have a different feeling with men."

"I don't care what your feelings are," my mother snapped. "You just haven't met the right girl yet. Mary Ann was too stuck up for you. She married a lawyer, didn't she?"

"Mom, really, it's not going to change. It's not about the right or wrong girl."

"But, John," my father pressed on, "do you know how hard your life is going to be?"

"Of course I know how hard life is going to be. But it would be worse the other way. I've tried pretending. Do you remember how miserable I was for a while in college? That's why. It was horrible. There were times I wanted to kill myself. At least this gives me a chance to find some happiness. And, besides, things are changing. That's why I'm writing this dissertation. Look at this gay studies course I'll be teaching. Things are changing, and I'm helping to make things change."

"But how can you be sure this is what you want? What kind of happiness are you going to find? You haven't found anyone yet. How can you know?"

"Dad, what do you mean there hasn't been anyone? Who do you think Billy was?"

"Billy!" My mother almost spit out his name. "We never liked him."

"Well, what about Carlos, then? You loved him! You liked having him over for dinner. You always asked about him. If he answered the phone when you called, you would bend his ear with

40

chatter. He built you that bookcase. Who do you think Carlos was?"

"Carlos?" I could almost hear them thinking. "But he moved to California this summer," Mom said.

"That's right. We broke up after four years. We couldn't make it work. It's been hard, and it was really hard not being able to tell you about it, but it was the right thing to do."

It was almost midnight. They wanted me to stay the night, but I knew I needed to get back to Manhattan, back to my own space, to breakfast in the morning at the West End, and the freedom to call my friends and report on the evening I'd just had. There were no buses in sight, so I started walking down Tremont Avenue, the tracks of the New Haven Railroad on one side of me. I mulled over each question and exchange. It hadn't gone badly, I thought. They were sure it was somebody's fault and it could be fixed, and that wasn't so good. But I didn't storm out of the apartment, and they didn't throw me out. Really, it could have been a lot worse. None of us lost it. I didn't get angry. We did keep talking. There weren't even any big shouting matches, in itself a minor miracle for the three of us.

At West Farms Square, I caught the IRT train to the west side of Manhattan. The rhythm of the train's motion and roar had a soothing effect, slowing down my mind and almost lulling me into sleep. It was then that I heard again my mother's parting comment as I kissed her goodbye: "I'll pray for you and Carlos."

"Oh my God," I thought, but this time the phrase had none of its usual edge of panic. "I don't know how long this is going to take, but I know that it's all going to be okay." Mom probably didn't realize it, but in that simple phrase she had accepted my relationship with Carlos. He was family, too. Carlos was included in her prayers.

Given the conflicting demands of God and family, Mom chose family and she was asking God for help.

For the next month or so, I returned home for dinner once each week. The discussions continued but, in a sense, I knew they were an anti-climax and that I was winning them over. Dinner by dinner, I could see their resistance wearing down. They put less and less heart into convincing me that I could change, that all this was temporary. They were resigned to an outcome that wasn't theirs to control. More and more in these conversations we'd slip off course and fall into patterns of small talk and easy laughter about events in the neighborhood or the parish. They were adjusting themselves to this new reality. And each encounter was less taxing on me. As I'd recount to my gay men's consciousness-raising group each Sunday night the latest installment of the D'Emilio family saga, I found myself settling into the conviction that, unbelievable as it would have seemed just a couple of months earlier, this was a gay liberation success.

Toward the end of the fall, after several of these dinners, they glanced at each other with that worried look I knew too well, and turned to me. Oh, boy, I thought, what are they cooking up now? Dad's tone was serious as he said to me, "John, your mother and I have been talking" (as if I hadn't known this!) "and we don't know how you're going to feel about what we have to say, but we really don't think we can keep this from the rest of the family. We just have to let everyone else know."

They could have knocked me over with a feather. I almost started to giggle with glee. They were going to make the rounds of aunts and uncles and cousins? They were going to call the family in California? They were going to save me the trouble of coming out by doing it all for me? And they wondered if this was okay? Will wonders never cease, I thought. I was thrilled.

Now the visits home took on an entirely different tone. They had become co-conspirators. After each coming out, they reported back to me. They described their calls to Anna and Lucy and Phil, their conversations at the dining room table on Silver Street with Jenny and Sylvia, the trip up to Westchester to tell Fran and Bill. They told me the questions that different family members had asked and how they answered. I had become the authority on my own experience, and they were asking my counsel. Who thought it could come to this?

After they were finished with Mom's family, they tackled Dad's. The D'Emilio sisters, Tessie and Annie, were a different breed from the Scamporlino girls. They were louder and shriller, always with an edge of panic in their voices no matter how innocent the topic of conversation, or how simple the issue at hand. Once, when I was about thirteen and my brother Jimmy was five, Tessie and Annie had come to visit us in Parkchester. I had recently received a reel-to-reel tape recorder as a gift, and Jimmy and I rigged it up so that, unbeknown to the adults, we could record their conversations. Later, after my aunts had left, we played it back for my parents. I suppose they could have taken offense, but instead the four of us were practically falling on the floor with laughter. At one point, Mom asked them whether they wanted tea or coffee and Annie replied "cuppa tea, cuppa tea, cuppa tea" in a tone that would have put Chicken Little to shame. For years after, if any one of us said "cuppa tea, cuppa tea," it provoked gales of laughter.

By this time, Tessie, Annie, and Annie's husband Felix, had left the old neighborhood on 147th Street and were living together in Bensonhurst, in a house owned by Felix's unmarried sister, Madeleine. Just as we used to take a cab down to the south Bronx to visit them every few weeks when I was a child, now my parents occasionally drove to Brooklyn to pay them a visit. Always the visit was arranged days in advance, and always they were on Sunday, when the traffic was lighter and they could drive during the day.

This time, probably because there was a tinge of anxiety on the part of my parents, they had called on a Thursday and asked if they could come by that evening. The next night, I was home for dinner, and they could barely contain themselves as they recounted what had happened. After everyone was settled into the visit and they were all having their coffee and cake, my Dad looked at them and, in what I'm sure was a somber tone, said, "There's something we have to tell you about Johnny."

Well, that did it. Before either he or Mom could get in another word, the three of them, Annie, Tessie, and Madeleine, too, began screaming: "Johnny, Johnny, Johnny! Oh my God! What's the matter with Johnny?"

"He's been in a car accident!"

"He has cancer!"

"He's on drugs!"

"He's been shot!"

At this point in the telling, my dad is now laughing out of control, holding his sides as he looks at my mom, who has picked up the thread of the story.

"Oh, John, you won't believe it. It was hysterical. Unbelievable! You should have heard them screaming. One thing after another they are shouting 'til, finally, your father and I start shouting back, 'no, no, everything's fine, there's nothing wrong, he's okay, he's just gay!'"

Just gay. That's all. No big deal. Not a problem. Could I have asked for a better outcome?

TRUTHS IN THE MIDDLE OF THE NIGHT
REMEMBERING AUNT FRANNIE

Charles Derry

The day my mother died, in 1976, my Aunt Frannie came over and spent the night. She kept asking me "Are you okay? Are you okay?" and I kept saying I was. She wore a flannel nightgown and slept in my mother's bed. I was twenty-five years old and had lost my father just two years before. With no brothers or sisters, I was now alone in the world, but I didn't really understand what "alone in the world" meant, at least not then. Instead, I was thinking that it felt good to have Aunt Frannie in the house, and that my father's death, which was still vivid, now seemed like a dress rehearsal for my mother's.

Through the picture window, I could see in the moonlight the Japanese maple that my father and mother had helped me plant when I was four years old and we had just moved into our little white box house in a Cleveland suburb. It had been my parents' first and only mortgage, and I had watched that exotic tree course into a spectacular life for twenty years, its leaves as red as blood. But now, with my mother gone, looking at it felt too sad, so I spent much of that first evening straightening the sofa cushions and re-arranging the knickknacks on the mantel. I had a complete, assembled collection of the Famous Monsters of Filmland: the Hunchback of Notre Dame, Dracula, Frankenstein, and Godzilla—all painted in gaudy colors with lots of blood and now collecting dust. "Are you okay, Chuckie? Are you okay?" asked Aunt Frannie from my mother's easy chair, and I said, again, that I was fine.

I didn't realize it then, but Aunt Frannie spent the night to make sure I didn't kill myself. Not that I was particularly moody, and not that I had ever hinted I could be capable of such an act. But Aunt Frannie knew about grief. She knew about despair in the middle of the night, and she knew the darkest and most profound truths because she had lived a long and complicated life. She knew that I was at risk even though I didn't know it. And maybe, just maybe, she knew that I was homosexual, though I had not yet acted upon it. I thought I was doing fine. Yes, Aunt Frannie, I'm doing fine, just fine.

Aunt Frannie was always old. Even when I was a little boy she seemed old. She was mannish, and not pretty, muscular in a stocky way that was perfect for stirring the vats of spaghetti sauce that seemed always to be simmering in her kitchen. She had three boys and an alcoholic husband who had been in prison more than once for acts that had since been cloaked in shame and silence. Sometimes I would spend weekends at her house in the old Italian neighborhood in Mount Pleasant, and her boys and I would take baths together in the same big tub where she would rub so hard I was afraid my skin would literally come off in the steaming water. "Ow!, Aunt Frannie, this water is boiling. You're cooking me!" "And skinning you, like chicken," she would say, and then tell me to be quiet as she rubbed even harder. On the shelves in her bathroom were bottles of violet-colored bath oils and perfumes: lavender, she told me. Yet their contents never diminished, and even as a little boy, I understood that the bottles were a fantasy she reserved for the future, not something she used. When would Aunt Frannie ever have had the time to luxuriate in a bath?

She was old when I was a little boy, and she was old in 1976 when I was trying to understand what it meant that my mother had died. Can you be an orphan at twenty-five, or was there some cut-off age? Because my mother's illness was so sudden, I felt shock more than grief.

It was as if my mother had been there, and now suddenly she wasn't; and in her place, at least for the night, was Aunt Frannie. So while I dusted my Phantom of the Opera model, I watched her, noting the vascularity of her arms, the alert eyes that looked so strange behind her trifocals.

"When was the last time your mother cleaned her floor?" asked Aunt Frannie, and I couldn't answer. And then, before I knew it, there she was, an old woman on her hands and knees, scrubbing the grey linoleum with a sponge and a bucket. "You can't use a mop if you're going to do it right. You have to use good old-fashioned elbow grease. Get close to the dirt!"

"Aunt Frannie, you're going to make holes in the floor, if you scrub that hard!" It was two in the morning and every light in the house was on and we were maniacs now in the guise of pretending to be getting ready for the relatives who would be bringing an Italian feast in a few days for the after-funeral meal. After a while, Aunt Frannie and I sat down in my mother's French provincial living room set from Value City, and Aunt Frannie told me calming stories about the twenties and thirties, the "old days" when she and my mother were growing up in Cleveland. They had always been so close.

The scene at the hospital had been anything but calm. I had been away at school in Chicago, working on my Ph.D. Although my qualifying exams had been scheduled for the next week, some strange impulse had prompted me to take them earlier, an impetuous act totally out of character. The moment I returned to my apartment to celebrate finishing my third twelve-hour day of exams, my mother, who didn't know how to drive, called to ask if I could come home to Cleveland. She was having pains in her back and needed to be taken to the hospital the next Monday for tests. Like Aunt Frannie, my mother never complained and never asked for help, so I knew, immediately, that something was happening too fearful to confront directly. I drove home the next day, and within a few hours of my arrival, my mother's face turned yellow and I rushed her to Marymount Hospital. Her decline was precipitous and mysterious and led to exploratory surgery two days later. After the surgery, the surgeon refused to talk to me in person and instead called me on a telephone in the waiting room. I could barely speak, so I just listened to his long monologue. Behind me stood Aunt Frannie, who was first in line to hear the news. And behind her stood so many others from my mother's huge Italian-American family that it's hard to remember who all was there: Aunt Jennie, Aunt Tannie, Aunt Frances, Aunt Fran, Uncle John, Aunt Florence, Uncle Ralph, and my cousins Joe and Gary and Donna, and Uncle Jerry and baby Jerry, and Uncle Frank and little Frankie, and Jerry's Frankie. And more.

Finally, I hung up the phone. When I turned around and saw all the faces looking at me, their eyes moist with expectation, I couldn't speak. On some level, it seemed that until I said the words, the words wouldn't really be true. Frannie served as the translator because all I could do was shake my head yes or no.

"Is the operation done?" asked Aunt Frannie.

A nod yes.

"Is she going to be okay?"

A sideways shake of the head.

"She's not going to be okay?"

Another shake no.

"What did they find?"

But that wasn't a question that could be answered without words, and pancreatic cancer could not easily be mimed. I did nothing.

48

"So how long will she live?"

Another impossible question.

"A year?"

A shake of the head.

"Longer?"

A shake of the head.

"Six months?"

A shake of the head.

"A month?"

Another shake of the head. Aunt Frannie took in a sharp breath of her own and continued on, steeling herself.

"A week?"

Yet another shake. And then, for a moment, my mother's face and Aunt Frannie's face seemed the same and I saw two little Italian girls sitting on the stoop on East 114th Street; and then Aunt Frannie was pressing forward, rubbing hard, not content until every piece of dirt was scrubbed from the skin, every piece of grime gone from that floor, her voice as sharp as the surgeon's knife:

"Less?"

Now, with an almost inhuman effort, I was able to remember how to produce sounds, could feel a rumbling in my throat and words gurgling up, then spitting out. But were they recognizable as words? It was a cry released:

"A few days."

Similar inchoate sounds had been coming from all my relatives; and Aunt Frannie, as the task-master, was keeping the despair at bay: the sniffling, the intakes of breath, and the low-pitched moans. But now, as Aunt Frannie gave out one involuntary gasp for her sister, for the shock, for the new way in which life would now be, the energy could no longer be contained: the volume grew, the pitch got higher, and suddenly everyone was shrieking, keening, the ululations

49

filling the room and echoing into a mass hysteria. I turned away from all of them.

The silence in the living room was broken now by the songs of early-morning birds.

"Are you sure you're okay, Chuckie?"

"Of course I am, Aunt Frannie."

"Well, let me make you some scrambled eggs."

It was always scrambled eggs for breakfast at Aunt Frannie's house. With black coffee, no sugar, no cream. She was the head of a family whose parents had died too soon, the oldest of eight brothers and sisters, the virtual grandmother to over twenty nephews and nieces. She had raised three sons; and when her youngest got a girl pregnant, twice, and didn't fully acknowledge the kids, she raised her grandchildren, too. Later, when her grandson got a girl pregnant and needed help with *his* baby, Aunt Frannie took in that little boy, too. At eighty-five years old, she was still changing diapers. Did I say already that she always seemed old? And yet she seemed inde-structible, too, beyond age.

Over scrambled eggs, she removed a bundle of holy cards from her purse. She had been attending funerals all her life, and those who had marched into their graves were now in her purse in four-by-two inch tombs—cards issued by Biondo and Sons Funeral Home, by Nosek and Sons Funeral Home, and by Ripepi Funeral Home. The images were beautiful: a luminous Virgin Mary with a glowing immaculate heart; Joseph in brown and blue, clutching a white lily and looking at the infant Jesus already gazing out with hope and compassion; Christ at the lugubrious Gethsemane; and Aunt Frannie's favorite, the weeping Virgin praying to God the fa-ther, a bush of thorns at her side, the crucified Jesus on Golgotha behind her, "In Loving Memory of...."

And then name after name: Martha Coshignano, Frank Monateri, James J. Iacano. It was the family, ever at hand: Aunt Bertha, Uncle Tony, Mary Cuppolina, Mary Pisa, with the words: "O gentlest Heart of Jesus, ever present in the blessed sacrament, ever consumed with burning love..." and "With the saints give rest, Oh Christ, to the soul of thy servant." She fanned out the dozens and dozens of cards; it was a deck of the dead.

I remember that my mother's obituary cost so much per word, and because there was so little money in my account or hers, I included little information. What did that brevity say about my mother? More notable was what was left out—truth and irony too unseemly for a public obituary: that she was an unassuming, intelligent woman who should have gone to college, but didn't because Italian women didn't need an education; that she sacrificed a majority of her adult life to take care of a sick husband, my father; that after making minimum wage working in a factory, she managed to mail in their last house payment exactly nine days before her death.

(Later, the paid-off mortgage arrived in the mail on the same day as the bill for her funeral.)

I remember, too, that Aunt Frannie came with me as I picked out the coffin, offering advice, but never insisting. She was a formidable presence as the funeral director extended his arm to shake my hand and she yelled at him, "You're *not* going to take advantage of my nephew! Don't even think about it! Do you hear me?" He withdrew his hand fearfully; we were going to be a tough sell. That was in 1976, and when I cleaned out my mother's house and finally sold everything, I threw out the Famous Monsters of Filmland models that my mother had so lovingly treasured on her knickknack shelves.

My mother wasn't around in 1978 to come to my Ph.D. graduation ceremony at Northwestern University. But Aunt Frannie helped to arrange for other family members to come to Chicago, so I wouldn't feel so alone. Aunt Frannie herself never traveled outside Cleveland: you never knew when there might be a funeral to go to, some old friend, some *paisan* from the old country. Besides, there were always kids that needed looking after.

Even that commencement ceremony seems like a lifetime ago, and now, when my students look at me, I am aware that many of them have long thought of me as old, the way I thought of my Aunt Frannie when, truth be told, she was still in the prime of her life. I wonder how many of my students can imagine me as young?

Once, in the middle of some dark night, when Aunt Frannie was finally irretrievably old, a drunk plowed his pick-up into her picture window, ending up in her living room on top of her easy chair. A third of her home was destroyed. Although she usually fell asleep in that chair, she had gone to her bed that night, spared that particularly traumatic end. She called 9-1-1, and then held the drunk at bay with a baseball bat, who was obstreperous in his delirium. Not only did she get a brand-new living room, but Aunt Frannie insisted on new porch steps, a wrought-iron railing, and new landscaping. "No one's going to take advantage of me!" she insisted assertively to the insurance company, even though there had never been a railing or landscaping before. "I could look pretty pathetic on the evening news complaining about your company!"

Also, not too long after, at a flea market in Middletown, Ohio, I came across a complete collection of vintage Famous Monsters of Filmland models like the ones I threw away, and each was selling for about a thousand dollars. How new they now looked to me: Frankenstein reaching out horrifically to grab you; the Phantom of the Opera removing his mask to reveal the terrible truth of his face while his tortured prisoner screams; the Hunchback cowering, his outcast's back whipped and bloodied, each lash more oppressive than the last; the Mummy enshrouded in white, for so long sleeping rather than living, resigned to his fate. Resigned. And to think that I had had a whole set!

I still dream about the knickknack shelves, their gaping emptiness, and wonder what the family who bought the house from me put on those shelves where my monsters had been. Or what was put there by the family that bought the house subsequently. Or the family after that one, or the one after that. Had there been other lonely gay kids working solitarily to create projects for a mom to display?

Yet, my gayness, which had once seemed so monstrous to me, like my models, had come to seem no big deal at all. My mother's death—go figure!—had served to unblock my fears, to wash them so thoroughly and clean away that I could accept myself.

Aunt Frannie was eighty-seven (or was it eighty-eight?) when she died of colon cancer, and she was still scrubbing her floor on her hands and knees shortly before she died. She was still filling in as a chef at the local Italian restaurant when the regular called in sick. She was still making Italian sesame candy, which required three hours of stirring at a hot stove. She was still making a hundred fifty pounds of Italian Christmas cookies every year and sharing some with me and my partner. And she was still changing diapers.

I thought about her and my mother when I was asked to give a commencement address at Wright State University, where I have now taught for over thirty years as an out, gay man. I was always a good teacher, I think, and the occasion for the speech was my having been given a faculty excellence award. Backstage in the dressing room as I was putting on my academic regalia, I discovered in my suit-jacket pocket the funeral card for Aunt Frannie: on one side was a beautiful picture of children praying to their vision of the Virgin Mary at Lourdes, on the other side an obligatory Bible verse intended to comfort. As I marched into the amphitheater of 14,000 people, I was overcome with feeling, almost unable to walk, and afraid I might also be unable to speak, like that time before, in the hospital.

Yet my words, inspiring, came easily. As I delivered my speech, I imagined my mother and Aunt Frannie listening in the amphitheater and wondered what they would have thought.

Certainly, neither would have communicated any effusive pride afterwards, just something simpler: "So how are you doing, Chuckie, are you okay? Happy with how it went? Good. Want to stop somewhere for some lunch? Maybe some eggs?"

Aunt Frannie's obituary, like my mother's, was in the *Cleveland Plain Dealer*, and it, too, had to be purchased at so many dollars per word.

But really, what does an obituary mean? And what does it impart about truths in the middle of the night?

FUORI IN ITALIA:
A GAY GRANDSON ENCOUNTERS
LA MADREPATRIA

George De Stefano

ROME, 2000

On July 8, 2000, my partner, Rob, and I marched through the streets of Rome with several hundred thousand gay men, lesbians, and our heterosexual allies. We were the shock troops of World Pride Roma, a week of gay cultural, social, and political activities that culminated in the march in Rome. But World Pride, an international celebration held in a different capital city each year, almost didn't make it to the Eternal City. The Vatican and its conservative political allies waged an angry, often unabashedly bigoted, campaign to prevent it from being held in Italy in 2000, the year of the Giubileo, the Catholic Church's millennial Holy Year celebration.

Truth be told, the event's opponents wouldn't have welcomed it during any year, at any time.

But the opposition to World Pride Roma generated an outpouring of support from Italians who believed that the attempts to ban it constituted an assault on the Constitution and *lo stato laico*, the secular state. A wide range of public figures offered their support, from the president of Rome's Jewish community to artists, such as filmmaker Nanni Moretti and playwright Dario Fo, as well as from leftist political parties, civil society groups, trade unions, and even grassroots Catholic organizations. The leftist newspaper *Il Manifesto* published a statement of solidarity with World Pride titled, "Siamo tutti gay."

World Pride Roma 2000 was a great success. Its significance, however, was greater than the size of the crowds or even the defeat of World Pride's formidable foes. What the event signaled was the refusal of the gay and lesbian community to accept the unfavorable terms of the social contract offered by Italian society. "In Italy, invisibility has been the price for tolerance," observed Sergio Lo Giudice, the then-president of Arcigay, the national gay rights association. "But gays don't want to be invisible anymore."

What has changed, however, is the greater visibility of Italian gays and lesbians since World Pride. The movement now is more outspoken and somewhat better organized, and gay issues enjoy more support from the general public. There even have been some political victories, with anti-discrimination measures and partner registries enacted by a few municipalities. Some openly gay men have won political office, the best known being Nicola "Nichi" Vendola, the twice-elected regional president of Puglia, and Rosario Crocetta, the outspoken leftist and anti-Mafia mayor of Gela, Sicily. In 2012, after having served two terms as Gela's mayor, Crocetta was elected president of the Sicilian Region, a position similar to an American governor.

But in general, the status of homosexuals in Italy lags behind the rest of Western Europe. The Catholic Church, and a family culture rooted in Catholicism, has created a climate in which far fewer gay men and women come out, build community, and engage in political activism. Catholicism may no longer be Italy's state religion, but its influence remains pervasive. Social attitudes towards homosexuality are strongly influenced by the Church's stance that it is both sinful and unnatural, and that gay people should be tolerated only as long as they suffer their condition in silence and don't demand civil rights or social acceptance. Most Italians don't heed the Vatican's diktats, and opinion polls consistently indicate general support for gay rights, including partner recognition measures. But the approximately 30 percent of the electorate whose political behavior is in synch with Church positions can influence the outcome of elections, especially close ones. Political parties of the right and center, and those center-left politicians known as the "theodems," cater to Catholic voters by opposing gay rights.

For most same-sexers, to use Gore Vidal's preferred term, Italy is very much the land of don't ask, don't tell. Don't tell your friends. Don't tell your co-workers. Don't tell your schoolmates. And for God's sake, don't tell your family; it would kill your mother. Given how often I've heard that one, Italian mothers must be a very fragile species indeed.

NEW YORK, 1980S

Growing up in a working class, Roman Catholic, Italian American family, this code of silence was one I knew well, that I lived by, and that conditioned my own path towards coming out and self-acceptance. I didn't acknowledge my sexuality to my family until I was in my late twenties and that breaking of familial *omertà* led to a period of estrangement from my parents. Fortunately, the estrangement was short-lived. But once I had come out, to myself, my friends, and my family, there was no looking back. The 1980s was the decade in which my identity as a gay man became fully articulated, in both the personal and public spheres. I met and fell in love with Rob, the man who, more than two decades later, remains my partner. I became an activist, involved with several left-of-center gay organizations. My journalism increasingly focused on gay topics. And when the plague of AIDS arrived, I joined the AIDS Coalition to Unleash Power, ACT UP, becoming one of those angry, obstreperous militants who confronted the Federal government, the pharmaceutical industry, the medical establishment, and the Catholic Church.

This was the personal history I brought with me when, in the 1990s, I first experienced gay life in Italy. My introduction to *la vita gay italiana* began with an encounter Rob and I had with a Sicilian university professor visiting New York. Gianni was very simpatico, intelligent, and funny. When he invited us to visit him in Catania, we eagerly agreed.

CATANIA, SICILY, 1995

During the summer of 1995, we spent several weeks in Sicily, a memorable trip on many counts. Gianni and his friends made sure we saw many of the island's most spectacular sights: Mount Etna and Mount Pellegrino, Taormina and Siracusa, the Moorish-Norman cathedral at Monreale, and the magnificent Roman mosaics at Piazza Armerina and Caltagirone, a town famous for its ceramics, where Gianni was born and his parents still lived. Gianni was also our Virgil, our knowledgeable guide to gay life in Sicily, both its sexual underground of cruising places—parks, beaches, movie theaters—and its small, organized gay community.

While I was in Sicily, so much reminded me that one side of my family originated on this island. My father's parents came from a town near Naples. So much felt familiar, especially the food and the way people looked and behaved. Visiting a grand old municipal building in Palermo, I was startled to see a woman security guard who looked remarkably like my mother did when she was young. During a lavish *pranzo* in the capital, our hostess, the mother of one of Gianni's friends, looked at me and exclaimed, "Occhi Siciliani!" (Sicilian eyes). One afternoon, as I lay on a hillside in Siracusa, overlooking the sea, basking in the intense sun, Gianni exclaimed, "Look, you blend into this landscape! You belong here!"

His comment amused and pleased me. But was it true? Did I belong there? As an American of Sicilian descent, I certainly felt an emotional connection to the place. But I felt something else as well; I felt a sense of disconnection, of not-belonging, and, at times, even alienation. That feeling was to recur on subsequent trips to *la madrepatria*, Sicily and elsewhere. As much as I enjoyed Italy, there always were moments when I felt the Italian and the American components of my identity clash, and, disconcertingly, this sometimes occurred when I was in the company of Italian gay men. The conflicts typically centered on family and religion, and the intersection of those two fundamental categories of Italian life with sexuality.

A few recollections—snapshots from fifteen years of my experiences in Italy—illustrate some of those conflictual moments.

I am nonplussed by all the religious imagery in Gianni's apartment: the holy cards, the portraits of the Virgin Mary, the little statues and other pieces that Rob, who is Jewish, calls "Catholic tcotchkes." Gianni affirms that he is indeed Catholic, adding, "But not the kind the Pope approves." I notice that among the arrangement of postcards on Gianni's bedroom door there is a picture of Padre Pio, the so-called mystic priest beloved by many Italians, especially southerners. Pointing it out, I say, with deliberate mischief, "Oh no, not that old fraud."

"What means fraud?" Gianni asks. I reply that Pio's so-called stigmata were self-induced wounds. I add that the veneration of Pio strikes me as a reactionary, superstitious cult. This does not go over well with Gianni. It will be only the first of our disagreements about religion.

LATINA, 2003

Luca, who Rob befriended in an Internet chat room, has invited us to visit him in Latina, a town south of Rome built in the 1920s by Mussolini. Luca, in his early thirties, has only recently come out. Just a few months earlier, Luca ended a lengthy engagement with Donatella, an interior decorator who designed his elegant apartment. On his dining room sideboard, I notice an assortment of framed photographs. One of them is of Pope John Paul II. I turn the photo against the wall. "What you done!" Luca exclaims, indignantly. I explain that it's weird for a gay man to revere such a homophobe. Luca agrees that the Vatican's anti-gay politicking is obnoxious, but he refuses to believe that the Polish pope is responsible for it. It must be the people around him, Luca insists. Well, there is Ratzinger, I acknowledge.

That evening, we are to have dinner at a place Luca calls "a real pizzeria napoletana." At the gate of his apartment complex, there is a small alcove that holds a statue of the Virgin Mary. As we drive past it on our way to the pizzeria, Luca makes the sign of the cross. I hadn't seen an Italian male do that since I was a child. I recall a trip to Yankee Stadium with my Uncle Joe and several of my cousins. On our way to the game, we drove past a Catholic church. My uncle and my cousins all made the sign of the cross. I didn't. At 12 years old, I already felt different from other Italian Americans I knew, acutely aware of my forbidden sexuality and the fact that I was not a believer. Now, in Italy, that sense of estrangement recurs. Except this time it's more pronounced. It wasn't surprising that my uncle and cousins would cross themselves. But a thirty-three year old gay man? In 2003?

NAPLES, 2000

Rob and I, along with our friend Miguel, are visiting Naples. Dario, another of Rob's Italian cyber buddies, has promised to "guest" us when we visit his city. Though nearly 30, Dario still lives with his parents, who do not know that he is gay. Unmarried adults are expected to live at home, and often, because of unemployment and scarce housing, they have few other options. Dario, who finds sporadic work as a computer programmer, falls into this social category. Dario's happy to spend a few days with his foreign guests because our presence provides an opportunity to get out of his parents' home and to be with his lover, Enzo, who is much older, perhaps 50. Over several days, we tour Napoli and its surroundings in Enzo's car, visiting the Amalfi Coast and Pompeii. On the day of our departure, Enzo and Dario drive us to the Naples airport. Dario gives us a warm farewell, but he seems a bit downcast. It's not hard to figure out why. After we leave, life will return to normal, or as normal as it can be to an underemployed, closeted gay man approaching thirty and living in a cramped apartment with parents and siblings.

Rob and I are struck by the fact that of our Italian friends, only one has come out to his parents. Luca's father died of cancer in 2008, and Luca never told him that he was gay. Salvo, a university professor in Catania, has had a long-term relationship with Michele, but he has never introduced him to his family. Gianni's partner of 10 years, another Salvo, whom we call Salvone ("Big Salvo") to distinguish him from the diminutive professor Salvo, lives with his widowed father and two sisters. He hasn't come out to them, and they think Gianni is just a friend.

Gianni is the only one of our friends who has not concealed his sexuality from his family, and his circumstances are unique, to say the least. Homosexuality, we learned, is a tradition in Gianni's upper middle-class family: his father and two of his paternal uncles were gay.

As a teenager just becoming aware of his own desires, Gianni had suspected that his father's sexuality wasn't exactly straight. For one thing, Papà had a succession of close male friends, younger men for whom he, a successful businessman, was employer and mentor. Gianni's suspicions were confirmed by a phone call to his parents' home. After the male caller heard Gianni's "Pronto!" he started talking dirty. Gianni laughed and said, "You must want my father." Silence, and then the line went dead.

When Gianni came out in his late twenties, his mother said, "Look, you can still get married and have kids. Your father was that way, and he got married." Gianni, to his great credit, refused to be part of this pervasive social hypocrisy.

Silence and invisibility, enforced by religion, family, and society—the oppression I'd rebelled against, and that American gay activists had undermined, still was commonplace in Italy. But on July 8, 2000, as we World Pride celebrants marched through Rome under a broiling sun, cheered on by throngs of spectators, it felt as if new possibilities were emerging. We met up with Salvo, who had come to Rome with a contingent from Sicily. With tears in his eyes, he said, "You have no idea how much this means to us."

SELINUNTE, SICILY, 2000

Two weeks later, Rob and I were in Sicily. Gianni and Salvone had planned a trip to Selinunte, an ancient town of Greek and Phoenician origins on the island's west coast. After the long drive from Catania, we arrived at our hotel, but as we checked in, there was a problem. Gianni had reserved two rooms with double beds, for Rob and me, and for him and Salvone. But the clerk decided that four men could not have accommodations with the "letto matrimoniale," literally: the marriage bed. He insisted we take rooms with single beds. Gianni refused to accept this. As the conversation turned into an argument, with rising decibels and growing frustration on both sides, the clerk's boss emerged from his office, quickly assessed the situation, and then sternly told his underling, "Let them have what they want."

Back in New York City, after an eventful Italian sojourn that began in Rome, went on to Naples, and ended in Sicily, we received an e-mail from Gianni. He said how much he and Salvone had enjoyed the time the four of us spent together. Then he put the confrontation with the hotel desk clerk at Selinunte in a different and surprising light. It turned out that the success of World Pride Roma, and the example of my and Rob's openness about our sexuality, had encouraged Gianni to challenge the disapproving clerk.

"Thank you," he said, "for bringing some of the spirit of World Pride to Sicily."

An Italian Honeymoon, 2011

The State of New York legalized same-sex marriage in 2011, a victory that was the fruit of years of activism by gays and lesbians and the indispensable support of New York's Italian American governor, Andrew Cuomo. Rob and I had been ambivalent about embracing an institution we regarded as a bulwark of heterosexist oppression, but once marriage equality was achieved in New York, we decided to get hitched. We'd been together 30 years and, our reservations about marriage notwithstanding, we resented the fact that our long-term commitment was denied the legal recognition that any heterosexual couple takes for granted. So, on July 24, 2011, the day marriage equality went into effect, Rob and I joined hundreds of other same-sex couples at City Hall in Manhattan, where we were married by a woman judge who proudly reminded us that, as a City Council member, she had been an early supporter of gay rights, including marriage.

We decided that we'd take our honeymoon in Italy, visiting Luca for a few days and then spending the rest of the two-week trip in Sicily. Gianni had advised us to arrive after the mid-August madness of *ferragosto*, vacation time in Italy, when most Italians, or at least those who can afford it, head to the seaside or the mountains. Gianni's counsel was wise; the weather in late August and early September still was sultry, but traffic on the *autostrade* was less congested, and beaches and other attractions less crowded.

On the first weekend of our honeymoon, Luca suggested we drive to Naples to stay overnight with Antonio, his new partner. To our surprise, our formerly closeted friend had come out to his widowed mother, and introduced Antonio to her as his partner. She took the news quite well. No fool, she had suspected for years that her first-born was gay. An artist and art restorer, Antonio lives in a *palazzo* (apartment building) in Cardito, a suburb of Naples. In his late forties, he is one of nine children his father sired with his mother and another woman. All his siblings live nearby, and in typical—or stereotypical—Neapolitan fashion, they are all intimately involved in each other's lives. Luca informed us that we would meet one of Antonio's brothers, Mario, the married father of two children, who had precipitated a family crisis by coming out of the closet.

After the four of us—Rob, Luca, Antonio and I—enjoyed a long, wine-fueled dinner of seafood antipasti and *spaghetti alle vongole*, Mario arrived. We had expected, and hoped for, a virile Neapolitan *maschio*, but Mario confounded our expectations, to say the least. He turned out to be one of the nelliest men we'd ever met. How, we wondered, did he ever pass for straight? How did he get a woman to marry him, and how did he impregnate her, not once but twice? We knew, intellectually, that gender presentation doesn't always align with sexual identity or behavior. That Mario was a flaming queen didn't mean he couldn't be a husband or father. But still...

Antonio told us that he was concerned about his brother's coming-out behavior; he feared that Mario was being sexually reckless, chasing after rough trade types he met in parks, arcades, and other cruising areas. Mario showed us photos, on his cellphone, of some of these men; we were impressed by his good taste. This newbie was as excited as a teenager who has just discovered the world of sex, but he was well into middle age, older than Antonio. We, like his brother, hoped that he wouldn't end up as a tragic cliché, one of those aging gay men taken advantage of, and even harmed or killed, by one of his pickups. But his enthusiasm for his new life was contagious. He felt he'd done his duty to *l'ordine della famiglia* (the family order, with its rules and obligations) by becoming a husband and father, and now it was time to really enjoy himself.

The next week, in Sicily, we reconnected with our old friends, whom we hadn't seen in five years, and made some new ones. With Gianni's apartment in the *centro* of Catania as our base, we returned to a number of our favorite places in eastern Sicily, mostly in the Catania area and the province of Ragusa, from which my maternal grandparents had immigrated to America early in the 20th century. During our stay, we were introduced to a new locale: Elloro beach, near the baroque city of Noto. The section of the beach—nude and gay—that we sought was a bit arduous to reach; we had to wade through small ponds and clamber over rocks and through trails thick with prickly underbrush before we reached our destination. But the trek was worth it. We arrived at a long strip of sandy beach full of gay men, most of them nude. We heard Sicilian accents, but also northern Italian ones, and other men speaking Spanish and French. Evidently word about Elloro had spread through the European gay grapevine.

The water was of a Caribbean blue color, the temperature warm, and the waves gentle. Men of varying ages, sizes, and shapes splashed each other, swam, and had playful sex—heads disappearing below the water's surface only to bob up seconds later. But not all the action at Elloro was aquatic. Gianni informed us that on a bluff overlooking the sea, there was an abandoned underground U.S. army bunker from World War II where men had sex. Rob and I had to see it for ourselves, but evidently our timing was off, as there were no cruisers to be found, just the evidence of their recent presence: discarded condom wrappers and crumpled tissues.

At Elloro beach, with its high sexual temperature, we luxuriated in what felt like a timeless, Mediterranean pagan sensuality. The Pope's anathemas and societal bigotry was out of sight, out of mind, especially while we were admiring a guy we dubbed "Superbear," a brown-skinned "moro" or "saraceno," bearded, muscular, hirsute, and hung, who, on that glorious afternoon, was the cynosure of our gaze, our Dionysius on the beach.

To celebrate Rob and me getting married, our friends arranged a couple of dinner parties, one at Gianni's family beach house at Marina di Ragusa, the other at Salvo's home in the town of Nicosia, near Mount Etna. Guests at the first party included a former professional soccer player (now a petrochemical engineer) and his partner, an older man from Milan. The ex-footballer and I prepared the seafood dinner. Gianni remarked, to my great pleasure, that my baked orata in *salmoriglio* sauce was easily the equal of and maybe even better than the version he'd had at one of Catania's leading *ristoranti*.

In Nicosia, at the house Salvo had recently bought and was still renovating, our host prepared a multi-course meal: antipasti, baked whole fish, and whole-grain locally made pasta with fried zucchini and ricotta. Gianni brought out the dessert, a *frutti di bosco* (wild berries) gelato cake frosted with cannoli cream. And on top of the cake was a figurine of two men, in wedding suits. I rarely smile in photographs, but in the pictures taken that night, my delight is unmistakable. Gianni dryly remarked that he bought the figurine on a recent trip to Germany, since such an item would not be available in Sicily.

Maybe someday, I thought, both, double bridegroom figurines and the social change they symbolize will come to this island, and to all of Italy.

JUST A PLAIN OLD (GAY) ITALIAN AMERICAN

Joseph A. Federico

I'm 100 percent Italian; my ancestors came from Calabria and Naples. My name is certainly recognizable, and I have a "Roman" nose. Great! Now what? Oh that's right, I'm also gay.

As I progress in life, I long more and more to learn about my ancestry; I want the full picture. Honestly, I cannot explain the gravitational pull toward this familial quest. When my last surviving grandparent died in 2011, I helped to empty out her apartment. What a dreary day that was. What I did not expect to find was a plastic folder filled with clues to my family's past. My grandmother's death clouded my judgment, as it should have, but I found my silver lining for the time being. The folder housed numerous American citizenship documents, school records, marriage licenses, and so on. Jackpot!

I have the beginnings of my family tree in my possession, but I can't help but wonder what they would have thought of me for being a homosexual. Would I fit in with them? Would I be spurned for being different? I'll never know.

I do know that I was raised right with very loving family members, and that's very important. Yolanda was my favorite grandparent. At around the age of 21 years old, I was in inner turmoil; I was in a deep depression about coming to terms with my sexuality, and did not know who to tell to free myself from the hell I was in. The first person that came to mind was my grandmother. I raced over to her house and spilled my innermost feelings. She sat there ever so calmly and did not have much of a reaction. She told me she loved me and nothing would ever change that. My grandmother also shared stories of suspicion of another distant relative being gay, and we got to the point where my news was accepted and put away for safekeeping. The rest, as they say, is history.

I come from a long line of hard-working masons; stone working and carpentry are in my blood. As a child, I enjoyed hearing stories from my father about trips and working excursions he'd been on with his father in the 1970s. I couldn't imagine being in the midst of tall skyscrapers in an inner city; I also couldn't imagine having to handle dry wall and be around asbestos for the majority of my life. When it comes to masonry, I think of one who breaks their ass to make a living and also one who creates for a greater cause. I can't help but associate myself with my Masonic ancestors; as hard-working as they were for their jobs, they struggled throughout their lives. I struggled, too, just in a different sense: with my sexuality.

I'm a gay Italian American man, but that doesn't make me any different than anybody else. I have hopes and aspirations of settling down after a fairytale wedding with the man of my dreams, and buying a house that comes equipped with a white picket fence and a two-car garage. Oh, and a child of each sex would be nice, too. Ah, to live the life of a dreamer.

I guess the moral of the story is that my family loves me for me, and the fact that I just happened to turn out gay didn't really make a lick of difference. I believe that everything happens for a reason, and being gay is no different than me having an Italian heritage. I'm proud to be a gay man, and also so very proud to be an Italian. *I sono tutto contente con il prefencia 'di' mai.*

MY IDENTITY IS LAVENDER, SO AM I ITALIAN AMERICAN?

Joseph Anthony LoGiudice

I was born on December 30, 1980, the day before New Year's Eve, at Maimonides Hospital, in Brooklyn, New York. My two Italian American parents, both in their early 20s, received their third child—me. My upbringing—more or less dysfunctional—centered on the neighborhood that I was raised in, Bensonhurst. It was a neighborhood known in the '80s for its large population of working-class Italian American people. As a Gay Italian American boy, and the youngest of three children, I always felt alienated and displaced living among a predominately heterosexual, Italian American community. Everyone around me ignored or rejected my seemingly atypical opinions and ideas because they did not follow the tradition. Living with a family that valued tradition immensely surrounded every aspect of my life. According to many Italian Americans and my family, tradition was marked by gender stereotypes, the practice of Roman Catholicism, the dependence on *la mia famiglia*, and the conformity to social norms. Over time, my individuality grew in momentum, and when I reached the age of 16, I developed the strength to rebel against everyone's expectations. I wanted freedom! My journey began with a train ride to Manhattan, or better known as "The City." People from Bensonhurst dubbed it "The City" because it represented everything outside of their comfort zone—and that was exactly what I sought. I craved the company of gay people. My gays, as I commonly referred to gay men, saved me from hating and destroying myself.

FAMILY HISTORY: AFFLICTIONS BEGIN

An abbreviated version of my family tree will give you a clear picture of my roots. The majority of my family members were descendents of southern Italy and Sicily. During the early 20th century, there was an insurgence of Italians bound for America due to Italy's decimated economy. My ancestors were not immune to these economic issues, leaving them no choice but to immigrate to New York City for a "better" life. From Bari, Napoli, Calabria, and Sicily, they landed on Ellis Island in New York City, and made a home in Brooklyn, New York. Mostly laborers, they lived and worked in Brooklyn, spoke a dialect of Italian in the home, and learned English to survive in America.

Immigrants who arrived in America during this time were ostracized for speaking broken or no English, subjected to intelligence tests, and discriminated against because of the color of their skin (usually an olive color) and body odor (they did not wear perfumes or colognes). Their first experience with discrimination began on Ellis Island, where American officials made it clear about their disdain for the Italians' foul body odors, negro-like appearances, ignorance of the English language, and poor aptitude scores. Some Italians returned to Italy by choice, or were not permitted to enter American soil. Although my ancestors endured these discriminatory experiences, they were able to enter New York City, and began building new lives for themselves. But these anti-immigrant experiences resulted in them isolating from the outside world. They created their own ethnic communities, usually filled with a variety of stores that would sell Italian goods, such as food and apparel; these places would become known as "mom and pop" shops, which continue to exist in Italian American communities. During my childhood, I could recall memories of my mother and I frequenting shops, which were owned by Italians who took great pride in their respective trades, from tailoring, butchering, shoe-making, barbering, and woodworking. From an outsider's perspective, it may appear that they enjoyed their new American lives, which were still very saturated with Italian goods and paraphernalia, but they maintained their paranoid personalities and fatalistic attitudes toward American life. Generations later, my family continues to manifest their ancestors' paranoid personalities, and to replicate the same fatalistic attitudes toward America.

FATHER, WHERE ART THOU?

Shortly before my birth, my parents were separated, and a year later, they were divorced. Their relationship was fraught with him cheating and her becoming acutely psychotic. My maternal grandmother, Nanny, became furious with my father's behavior, and evicted him from our apartment. His presence never made any difference to us because he was unemployed, lazy, and selfish. Incapable of caring for himself, he turned to his parents, who resided in Long Island, New York, to live with them. Anything he did was like an act of God to his parents; they treated him like royalty. After losing their eldest son to a tragic construction accident (an accident which they profited from by collecting a huge sum of life insurance money, which then afforded them the luxury of moving from the Marlboro Projects, in Brooklyn, to upper-class Long Beach, Long Island), they were unwilling to cut the umbilical cord with their younger son, my father. But he was always a pathetic excuse for a father and a human being, never once considering how his behavior affected my mentally ill mother and his children. While my mother was in her most vulnerable state, he infrequently visited our apartment, in order to have sex with her. The mere thought of his selfishness and ability to exploit a mentally ill person makes my stomach turn.

"IF NOTHING IS GOING WELL, CALL YOUR GRANDMOTHER." — ITALIAN PROVERB

Nanny, the person whom I value the most in life, always placed us children as a first priority. While my mother and father were having difficulties with finding an apartment, Nanny secured one for us, which was located down the hall from her apartment. But after my father was gone, my mother's mental illness began to snowball in severity, leaving Nanny worried about her daughter's ability to care for us. Neighbors and teachers telephoned Child Protective Services (CPS) to report neglect. Workers from CPS visited our apartment on two occasions. During one of those visits, I was home from school and witnessed the worker asking questions: Why were we home from school, why was our apartment unkempt, why were we disheveled, and what was my mother's perception of these issues? At this point, she was so far gone in her psychotic reality, which was indicated in her answers: "It's fine. There's nothing wrong."

These two incidents alarmed Nanny to step in as the primary caregiver. Nanny watched us with a close eye. She ensured that we had clean clothes and food, that we attended school, and that we had plenty of affection. And from time to time, Nanny gave our apartment a heavy duty cleaning and organized all our items, so neighbors would no longer say it was a safety and hygiene issue. My mother's illness slowly stabilized since Nanny monitored her psychiatric appointments and the administration of her medication. Every night, Nanny would call my mother's name from down the hall, and say to her, "Anna, you gotta take your pills!" Nanny always prompted us to do our daily chores and functions; it all began in the early morning: first a phone call in the morning to wake us up for school,

73

then making sure we ate breakfast before heading to school, then calling us after school to find out if we needed any essentials, then eating dinner with her, then watching television with her, and concluding with a goodnight kiss.

I could tell Nanny was drained most days from working full-time in the City and then having to arrive home to her second job—that of caregiver. Nanny was also a single mother of three children after she kicked her husband out for cheating on her while my mother was still a teenager. Left to her own devices in the late '60s, Nanny, at the age of 35, found herself monetarily broke with three children, living in her ex-husband's family's house, with only one option: find a job. Thus, she looked through the newspaper, and luckily landed a secretarial job at MetLife Insurance, a job she would have for her entire 30 year career. Ironically, she was the only one in the family who was not Italian American. Nanny's values were learned from her Greek-immigrant father, who cared deeply for the well-being of his family. Similarly, he worked round-the-clock to ensure his children were feed, housed, and dressed. Without her, my life would have been inconceivably plagued by several overwhelming circumstances.

There are always those people who will accept you in spite of the dominant cultural beliefs and practices. For me, Nanny was this person. She displayed great affection and interest in my persona, never once criticizing me. It did not matter to her that I wore non-gender conforming clothing (some would call it gay club attire) and that my voice was high-pitched. She tried to protect me from being bullied, especially when I endured slander at school and in the neighborhood. Many times, I arrived home crying, feeling such a great deal of despair. I immediately ran to the telephone, in order to call her at work, and tell her what transpired. Even while she was busy at her job, Nanny carved out time to comfort me with kind words. In comparison, she contended with the Italian Americans who did not believe that women should work and divorce their husbands. And then to add a mentally ill daughter and gay grandson to the mix resulted in Nanny being relegated among these people. Her compassion, empathy, conviction, and strength of character were strong enough to surmount these realities. Nanny would not allow a backward-thinking neighborhood—and conservative society—to oppress her. This is the kind of strength that taught me to persevere.

YOUR AVERAGE ELEMENTARY SCHOOL ENVIRONMENT: MY FIRST EXPERIENCE WITH HOMOPHOBIA

My first experience with homophobia occurred in the early ' 80s at a public school located a block away from our apartment. When I was in the fourth grade, my peers decided to publicize their attitudes toward gays after an incident in the gymnasium. They were playing relay races (a stupid game that fostered competition and always ended up with someone injured), while another boy and I were lying on the sidelines. I impulsively jumped over him, and we made body contact. Our peers observed, with their little beady eyes, our body-to-body contact. Subsequently, we were escorted from the gymnasium to the classroom, and then all of them ganged up on me and the other kid. They yelled "gay boys" at us for the rest of the day. During this slander, our teacher was in the hallway, gossiping with another teacher.

The rest of my grammar school experience surrounded homophobic slurs. When a fellow student came in close contact with me, they would say in the nastiest and cruelest tone, "eww, fag, get away from me!" No one talked to me. From that day on, I cautiously preceded through school. I was afraid to be myself. No one protected me. And yes, I was gay. And he was probably gay, too, but that did not give them the right to discriminate against us. Who taught these kids how to hate gays? Their fears of homosexuality were projections of attitudes learned from others. These homophobic experiences are etched so deeply into my memory.

I ran home to tell Nanny about this incident. I described to her what happened, but did not display any emotion (a common outcome from experiencing trauma). Nanny decided it was time to have a discussion with the teacher. During an open house at the school, Nanny visited my negligent teacher, Ms. Levine, to ask why she did not protect me. Ms. Levine avoided the question, focusing instead on my academic issues and personal problems. She should have aggressively addressed the homophobia with the class; it was in her power to look after all of her students—not just the students who she valued more than others (usually those students with higher test scores). Teachers are taught in their teacher education programs about multiculturalism as a teaching protocol; it is a way to promote healthy development and respect for others' identities. Then, why did Ms. Levine evade this responsibility? Ms. Levine's negative reports affected how future teachers treated me in grammar school: like a dumb, pathetic, white, Italian American boy from Bensonhurst. Typically, teachers never asked me to answer questions and assigned a seat for me in the back of the classroom. Their misperceptions further incited rage and anger, but these feelings were bottled up. Thus, I became completely dissatisfied with education and its environment, and then developed a high level of mistrust. Ms. Levine's behavior was both inexcusable and reprehensible.

The beginning stage of internalized homophobia emerged from this early experience. Others' fears of homosexuality were interjected into my own inner world, resulting in hate turned against myself, and the development of low self-esteem. Other residual effects were relentless thoughts of worthlessness, feelings of helplessness and hopelessness, and depressed and anxious moods. These effects endured throughout young adulthood when I began participating in drinking and partying habits, and having anonymous sex.

I was classified as a deviant person because of my homosexuality. Commonly, when people are afraid of others who they believe are different, those people label them as misfit, outsider, deviant, crazy, weird, and abnormal; these labels act as a form of discrimination, denigration, and marginalization. These labels have major implications that are much more severe on the receiver, who is of inferior status in the hierarchy of domination and subordination. But the psychological consequences are perhaps the more devastating part, whereby the receiver internalizes their connotative meaning and exhibits clinical symptoms. In examining their influence on my life, they made me feel ashamed and embarrassed to be the person who I am. Like Alan Downs described in his book, *The Velvet Rage*, I exhibited obsessive compulsive behavior from feeling such shame. Since the memories don't ever fade away, the byproduct is profound wounds on my psyche, and regressions of maladaptive thoughts and behaviors.

The ongoing verbal abuse that I suffered falls into the category of trauma. If a trauma is not offset by positive coping and social support, it leads to destructive effects on the psyche. One of my ways to cope with the trauma was to unconsciously detach from it emotionally, which is an instinctive response for victims. The re-experiencing of these traumatic, homophobic occurrences taught me that our society did not sanction boys/men touching, kissing, or demonstrating any emotional or sexual attraction toward one another. By no means is this an atypical story for gay men: several stories describe the verbal and physical abuse, and the lack of social support necessary to buffer how these experiences effect their development. It is documented in social science literature that youth who endure homophobia in school develop risk factors, such as suicidal behavior, absenteeism, depression, and anxiety. These youth are also at the greatest risk for suicide.

In a similar vein, ethnic and minority communities are unfortunately familiar with the effects of discriminatory experiences because they, too, are victims in our society. In their literature and in the media, narratives speak of marginal status, racial and sexist epithets, and the institutions that prevent them from gaining social and economic mobility. However, the difference is that these communities provide social support to their abused members. Consequently, they develop the resiliency to bear these experiences, which do not puncture their self-esteem. Gay men contend with greater adversities; they are treated with contempt because of their lack of conformity, and ostracized and alienated by their own families and communities. To save themselves from these hellish experiences, they separate from their past and relocate to a gay or gay-friendly neighborhood where they can cultivate their identities. But some of us may not reach adulthood.

INTERMEDIATE SCHOOL: A SAFE HAVEN

The misery that I endured in grammar school relented when I entered intermediate school; this gave me the opportunity to start fresh by creating a new circle of friends. Within the first month, I befriended many students who seemed to care about my "otherness," and in many ways they resembled me. They gave me the courage to care about myself, which was the catalyst for changing my perception of the school environment. I put a lot of effort into school work. Formally known as the "C" average student, I was earning "A's" in my classes. In the first month of school, I earned the "Student of the Month" award, which was given to the top achieving students. Shock was my initial reaction. Why was everyone treating me better? I was in such disbelief that I actually forgot to attend the pizza party in honor of the recipients. That year proved that I was not the stupid, faggot, Italian American boy, from Bensonhurst; such stereotypes of people are harmful to their personal development and can negatively affect many aspects of their lives, including school. My stellar performance earned me a spot in the honors program in the seventh grade.

The assumption from outsiders may be that I regained the ability to cultivate my identities from the positive experiences in intermediate school, but that was not the case. In reaction to past events, a false identity arose that disguised my true self. This identity excelled in school, compensating for the lack of confidence, praise, and validation that I did not receive from my other identities, causing a fracture in my self-concept. This false identity quickly turned into a mastermind, academically, which stole all of the leadership roles for the school newspaper and student clubs, and earned several honors and awards. Although this false identity garnered praise in school, the inner me felt silenced and afraid of coming out. My peers in school could not detect the feelings of shame, embarrassment, fear, loneliness, and rejection that persisted internally as a result of the trauma in elementary school. It is not uncommon to find gay men, like me, who excel in school because it is a means of achieving a level of self-acceptance.

BENSONHURST:
NOT EXACTLY A GAY-FRIENDLY NEIGHBORHOOD

The neighborhood I grew up in, Bensonhurst, was deeply conservative, so it was essential to manifest typical male behavior. Secondly, as a man of the Italian American community, gender conforming behavior always played a major role. The macho Italian American guy—the paternalist, the breadwinner, and staunch believer of the Italian American experience—made me feel uncomfortable and undesirable. I was the antithesis of this model. My natural affinity was to play with dolls, style my hair, adorn myself with female apparel, and engage in "girly" sports, like hop-scotch and jump rope. My high-pitched voice was another noticeable stigma, which people associated with gay men, compared to other Italian American boys with their deep masculine voices. The boys would call me every name in the book: fag, gay-boy, gay-lord, and girl. The girls did not think I fit in either. If they were to play with me, then the boys may perceive them as weird and unlikeable. So, my few friends were the other outcasts and unpopular kids: the girl whom no one else liked; the other effeminate boy.

During my early to middle adolescence, I made a concerted effort to masculinize myself. I played "masculine" games, watched sports, and became acquainted with male friends. And it was not unusual for me to fantasize sexually about those male friends. But my shame continued. The few boys who I became friends with were probably gay, too, but fearful to admit, acknowledge, or analyze it. Vinnie and Anthony, both Italian American boys, were close friends of mine, who strangely seemed to have the same effeminate behaviors that I displayed. How we managed to find each other is still a mystery to me. Could it be that my "Gaydar" was fully functioning at 13 years old?

After some time, it became exhausting to adhere to their expectations. My male peers and teachers forced me to engage in baseball, football, and basketball, which I adamantly refused to participate in, or was too "ill" that day. If I didn't comply, they made a mockery out of me. I hated all of them for attempting to control my behavior.

My attempts to fulfill the male gender stereotype failed, and I was regarded as, and called, a "sissy" or a "girl" (sadly reflecting their negative stereotypes of women) by people in the neighborhood and in school. My otherness made them uneasy. The pain of everyone's rejection penetrated my soul. In the short term, conformity may have been tempting, but I chose to preserve my identity.

HOME LIFE: NOT A WHITE PICKET FENCE

As if being a Gay Italian American boy was not bad enough, I also struggled with personal issues at home. The only competent person to care for my needs was Nanny—but my mother, who was diagnosed with paranoid schizophrenia, was left alone with us kids during the day time. Most days, she would sit in the dark, alone, talk to herself about people stealing clothes from her, dress herself in theatrical clothing, and sing Madonna songs. During my younger years, her psychotic episodes were more frequent. None of us understood how to address these behaviors. When Nanny would get home from work, she would yell at my mother for acting foolishly and speaking insanity. Nanny was embarrassed by her, and confused by her condition. We children did not make it any easier. We would yell, scream, run around, and lament about something. In the poor mental state she was in, my mother always showered us with affection. Every day, she kissed our cheeks and told us how much she loved us.

Throughout the years, my mother entrusted me with the parental responsibilities and she relied on me to combat others. Her illness made it impossible to work, manage the finances, and maintain our apartment. We battled each month to pay for the basic necessities since we depended on public assistance and it was minimal. We knew our mother had an illness; and the people in the neighborhood and at school knew, too. During an intense psychotic period, my mother was obsessed with wearing provocative clothing and black eyeliner all around her eyes, and leaving her coarse curly hair in knots; this was how she would take my sister and me to school.

We were embarrassed and worried about what others would say. And people would say the most despicable things about her. At the supermarket, Welfare Center, and utility company, people responded to her with dismissive and scathing remarks, and this was when I interjected with nasty and scolding words.

THE ITALIAN AMERICAN COMMUNITY: TRADITION HAILS

On a study abroad experience in Madrid, Spain, in 2003, I passed by a church that was inscribed with: "Anything that is not tradition, is the plague," which explains my experience of growing up in an Italian American community. Their beliefs, values, morals, expectations, and practices were imposed on me. The way in which the Italian Americans conveyed their expectations was through investigative tactics, beginning with intrusive questions that demanded answers conforming to their belief system. From childhood, and until late adolescence, the Italian Americans insistently probed me: "When will you get married Joey? When will you have children? When will you buy a house in the neighborhood? What type of work will you do?" Honest me, I responded with "I don't know," which did not please them. And then they asked the same questions over, and over, and over. What should I have said to them? Was it not obvious that I was gay? I thought my high-pitch voice was enough to tell them that a wife and children were not in my near future. They were suffocating.

I observed the traditional milestones of my fellow Italian Americans and it became clear the path that they would follow. First, they were born to an Italian American family where the father was the breadwinner of a blue-collar business and the mother stayed home bare feet. Their children would attend Catholic school and observe all the holidays associated with that religion. As they reached adulthood, they were expected to follow in the same footsteps as their

82

parents. A man would work for his father's business, get married, purchase a house in the neighborhood, have children, and behave according to the religious and cultural beliefs. For a woman, she would immediately be paired with a man, get married, have children, and manage the household. There was no room for flexibility. Object Relations theorists posit that separation and individuation are vital for healthy development, but for Italian Americans, no such a theory of development existed for them. To separate from their family, create their own value system, and generate new norms and behaviors was unconscionable. Thus, my lack of conformity to these beliefs, practices, values, and expectations made my Italian American family and community think of me as superlatively queer.

If you have not already figured it out, the Italian American community firmly denounced homosexuality. An example elucidates their homophobia, heterosexism, and racism: Every year, during the summer time, a feast was hosted by the neighborhood Roman Catholic Church; it was a fundraiser and a way to bring the Italian American community together. Each year, my family and I attended, but when I reached late adolescence, I enjoyed the company of my high school friends, so they joined me in celebrating one of the feasts. Although my friends and I poked fun at the provincial, pious Italian American folks who attended, none of us felt comfortable around them. We were a diverse group of people from Mediterranean, Latino, African American, Indian, Middle Eastern, and Asian backgrounds. We felt out of place, especially when the people gave us disapproving stares.

A young, Italian American man with a thick Brooklyn, Italian American accent accosted me at the feast: "You might as well wear a dick on your arm." I was embarrassed and ashamed. My face turned red and I walked away from him, scared to stand up for myself. My friends who were standing around me didn't know what to say either. I looked at myself again, and thought: "Do I look too gay?" I was wearing a brightly colored shirt, which was fitted tightly to my body, and bell-bottom jeans. Was I being too obvious about my sexual orientation? Why did my appearance bother him? I understand this young (heterosexual) male was fearful of my homosexuality. He was probably having issues with his sexual orientation. Always the men who have to make comments are the men who are queer themselves. But why did other Italian Americans, who overheard the comment, not step in to diffuse the situation? Obviously, Italian American or not, homosexuals were not deserving of their help. This type of hatred toward homosexuals is learned in the Italian American community. If you fast forward to today, which is approximately 16 years later, the mainstream media broadcasts Italian Americans on reality shows, or in politics, and or in powerful positions making derogatory comments about gay people. The Italian American community needs to overcome their traditional attitudes and adopt an inclusive platform!

TO BE RELIGIOUS—OR NOT

Like many gay men, religion was a source of constant tension for me. My Italian American family and neighborhood followed the customs of Roman Catholicism. As a child, I had no authority in making decisions, and was ordered to attend Catechism classes, where I would eventually receive Holy Communion and Holy Confirmation. Every dreary Wednesday afternoon, I sat in a classroom with approximately 25 Italian American boys and girls who attended private Catholic schools, and dressed in their school uniforms. We learned about the Bible, and God's desire for us to be moral beings (boring!). Many of the students never acknowledged my presence, and to them I represented a poor, gay, Italian American boy from public school. In their view, I was sloppy, ignorant, and effeminate, and did not deserve their attention. No one talked to me. Of course, I felt like an outsider. I sat in my chair, quiet, sad, alone, depressed, and feeling useless around my peers and teacher. I was openly discriminated against because I did not conform to their ways—the Roman Catholic, heterosexual, middle-class ways. I desired to be accepted by others, and yearned for their affections and attention.

I never understood why my relatives were "devoted" Roman Catholics. Take a look at my father's family: they hardly attended church, never read the Bible, and they broke several commandments, daily. They cursed, lied, and manipulated one another. They did not respect one another, which was displayed at family gatherings and during holidays. All of my memories are of them yelling at each other at the dinner table, and talking about their unhappy, unfulfilled lives.

During one Christmas Eve, my siblings and I went to my father's parents' house to celebrate the holiday. This was a rare occasion because we always spent Christmas Eve with Nanny. Rather than enjoying the holiday and focusing on why we celebrate Christmas, my father's family gossiped about the size of people's houses in Long Island. My grandmother, who was always jealous of everyone's wealth and looks, would make comments, such as: "Why doesn't my house look like that? Did you see what she looks like? She's a phony." My father's family always had hang-ups on wealth, materialism, appearance, status, and class (remember: they moved from an apartment in "the projects," to a fully detached house in upper-class Long Island). They even had the audacity to talk negatively about Nanny at the dinner table. "Your Nanny thinks she is better than us!" my grandmother exclaimed while twitching her head (such a drama queen). This was not the first time that she made nasty comments about Nanny. I hated her for making these comments. But I sat silently because I did not want to get into an argument. When we didn't respond to her comments, she would go into a rant about how we kids were ungrateful, and that she kept all the receipts from the clothes they purchased for us (pretty insane, right?). My paternal grandmother was jealous of the relationship that we had with Nanny. Since we lived in close proximity to Nanny, it was only natural that we were closer to her.

After we departed from my paternal grandparents' house, my siblings and I discussed our feelings of disdain toward our father's family. We resented the comments made about someone we loved and cared for deeply. If I remember, we decided to never return to their house. The most confounding part was that they called themselves Catholics. My father's family was particularly dysfunctional, the kind that one is embarrassed by to the point of contempt. What a gross hypocrisy to call them Catholics.

To complicate my life further, my partner's family is devout Roman Catholic. But like my family, his *famiglia* does not know why they are religious, except that it is a part of tradition. It is my belief that many Italian American families have difficulty with breaking away from their customs. Their conservative impulses are overwhelmingly pervasive, permeating several parts of their lives. Although my partner and I have broached the subject of transcending these beliefs with our families, they get scared and upset. Then they start calling us serious. Several times we have had fierce debates or heated arguments on Roman Catholicism. My partner and I accept who they are and what they believe in, but in our private lives, we live according to our own beliefs.

Although I do not speak for every Gay Italian American man, it seems obvious that Roman Catholicism rears its ugly head into many of our lives, and causes us to move further away from our families and communities. There are Gay Italian American men who do not have a relationship with their fanatically religious families. In a world that no longer heeds ignorantly to the demands of a religion, I question why people hold on tightly.

SEXUAL ENCOUNTERS: DON'T ASK, DON'T TELL

From the ages of 13 until 16 years, I was stuck in an awful sexual relationship with my brother's friend, an Italian American named Angelo. Angelo was approximately three years older than me, with dark features, and olive skin. I will always remember Angelo's big brown eyes and dark, thick hair. He was very handsome and well endowed. He always struck me as strange because of his quiet nature, which I attribute to latent feelings and thoughts of homosexuality. He kept a distance. That distance did not exist between us. Angelo could hide from his true identity—his homosexuality—because he engendered the male gender stereotype. He participated in sports, dressed in a rugged manner, played and hung out with the guys, and his voice was very deep.

I knew Angelo was gay, and that he wanted me sexually. Most of our interactions were sexual, and our conversations minimal. The days and nights that we came together to have sex, he pretended to be sleeping while it all happened. Our "relationship" was silly, and honestly, not something that I would call a relationship today. We did not share each other's lives. We goofed around with each other and had oral sex. The sex was boring, too.

Angelo was able to mask his homosexuality from everyone. Therefore, he did not embrace this identity. Angelo was aware that his Italian American community and family would only accept a heterosexual man. His internalized homophobia ran deeper than my own. Conversely, I could not hide from my auditable stigma—my voice—which actually aided in developing a strong sense of self. Rumors surfaced that Angelo abused drugs and had no direction in life. He never came out of the closet.

At 16 years old, I called it quits with Angelo. The oral sex was not fulfilling because I wanted a relationship. I made the monumental decision to leave the neighborhood and go to The City to meet gay people. It was time to be out of the closet and remain out.

THE CITY: THE GAYS SAVED ME!

I was afraid to travel to Manhattan because of all the paranoid things that my family and neighbors said about it: "Joey, be careful of the City. Aren't you afraid of being alone? Why do you want to go there? It's dangerous. People are weird. You can get mugged. The trains are not safe." To travel to the City, alone, was scary, but worth the effort. Upon arriving to Greenwich Village, a gay man directed me to the Gay and Lesbian Community Center; he said that it would be the best place for me to meet other gay youth. When I entered the Gay and Lesbian Community Center, looking like a damsel in distress, the front desk immediately asked how they could help me. I was led to Youth Enrichment Services (Y.E.S.), a division that provided support services for gay youth in the City. A staff person invited me to attend the BiGLTYNY (Bisexual, Gay, Lesbian, Transgender Youth of New York) group weekly, where I could talk about anything.

Every week, I made the journey to the group, and finally began cultivating my gay self: it was heard, manifested, and explored. Soon enough, I started attending the men's group, too, weekly. In groups we discussed issues ranging from discrimination in school, overcoming trauma, developing coping skills, and embracing oneself. Our groups felt like a "pick-up" because the boys and girls were eager to engage in sexual activity. After weeks of being involved in groups, I bonded with several of the members. After group ended, we would stroll throughout Greenwich Village and Chelsea, singing Madonna songs with our high-pitch voices, voguing, eating pizza, dancing with other queens on the Piers, and drinking alcohol to cope with our unfortunate realities. They were my pillars. These were some of the best times of my life. At last, I was free to be me.

RESTORING MY ITALIAN AMERICAN IDENTITY

The fall of 1999 marked a new chapter in my life with the start of college. On the one hand, it was liberating to live independently on the Upper West Side and attend the school of my dreams. Conversely, I contemplated why a void existed in my soul. My self-concept was disconnected: the gay self was robust whereas the Italian American self was fragile. Such a disconnect led to feelings of emptiness, and ways to avoid it were by drinking more than two times a week, meeting men at clubs in Chelsea, and objectifying myself. Drinking and having anonymous sex temporarily filled the void when it became too overwhelming to cope with.

In the sophomore year, emptiness turned into depression, and the drinking and sex were getting out of control. This is when I finally sought psychotherapy at the University's counseling office. A clinical psychologist was assigned to me; she was a kind person who tended to my issues with extraordinary care. The focus of our sessions were symptoms of depression and anxiety, and reasons why drinking were filling my void. We talked about my past, including the homophobia from the Italian American community, and we developed solutions to restore my ethnic identity. On the weekends, I visited my family in Brooklyn and I realized how important my Italian American traditions, behaviors, and practices were to me.

At Columbia, I joined the Italian American group, Societa Italiana. The group consisted of ten students, which was a small student group compared to the other ethnic/cultural groups at the University. We spoke endlessly on the traditions, behaviors, and practices of Italian Americans, but nothing on Gay Italian Americans. The discomfort of addressing queer issues was conveyed to the students through the University. The University refused to make queers a part of the academic curriculum. Being queer was a private issue.

After graduating, I moved in with Nanny. I was unemployed and felt helpless and hopeless. Instead of recidivating, I spent the leisure time writing in a journal and reading books. These new coping mechanisms were learned from years of therapy. There was the ability to self-exam and self-reflect on my history and identity. After reviewing these journal entries, I discovered the questions that were at the heart of the problem: What did it mean to be a Gay Italian American man? Why was I still facing the issue of acceptance? And whom could I rely on for support and understanding?

BACK TO BENSONHURST: FINDING THE LOVE OF MY LIFE

Upon returning to Bensonhurst, I befriended a few Gay Italian American men, whom I met at a gay bar in the Bay Ridge neighborhood of Brooklyn. They would help me to meet the man of my dreams, Michael Carosone. It was October of 2004 that I met Michael accidentally in a traffic jam in Manhattan. I was heading to the City to meet a friend for dinner and to go see an independent film. On my way to the City, I was re-directed to another road because of a parade, and so I ended up in Tribeca. Bored and stuck in traffic, I looked outside my window to discover two of my gay friends from Brooklyn in the car next to me. I yelled out of the window "Hey!" They were surprised that I was also stuck in traffic with them in the City. My friend, John, said they were going to the Gay Erotic Expo with Michael, who was driving. "Who's Michael?" I yelled. John said I didn't know him because he was a homebody. The bumper of Michael's car, which had already caught my attention, was decorated with stickers that advocated for vegetarianism, gay rights, and animal rights. The Italian flag and Gay Pride Rainbow flag also adorned the bumper. Our conversation was abruptly ended because the traffic cleared, and so we said our goodbyes with the intention of meeting later that night for coffee. At 11pm, we met at a restaurant in Gramercy. I finally had the pleasure of seeing and talking to Michael in person. The night was short, and we didn't get to talk much (and I didn't exactly make the best impression).

The next night, I met Michael at his apartment in Marine Park, Brooklyn, for a cup of coffee and conversation. That night, we hit it off. We shared so many stories, on men, family, Italian Americanism, food, school, Brooklyn, and relationships. Six weeks later, we were living together, and sharing each other's lives. Michael was instrumental in helping me to embrace both identities and thrive for a positive existence. The sharing of our personal stories showed the universality of our experiences. Thus, this enabled me to move beyond the past and live in the present. His love and support influenced me immensely, and we are best friends and partners.

Although the past no longer haunts my present reality, those memories remain—and they will never be forgotten. To recount these experiences has been a difficult process for me, but the reason for writing this personal essay was far more compelling than anything else: to uncover the homophobia that exists both in school and in the Italian American community, and to illustrate the effects of internalized homophobia.

In these contemporary times, I am still reading, hearing, and watching stories about the physical and verbal abuse that gay men endure from others. Schools have not instituted a queer curriculum, and the Italian American community rejects their queer members. I wonder if this essay will change their minds.

A Gay Guido's Pilgrimage:
Remembering Rome's 2000 World Pride

Michael Luongo

There's a fine line between gay and guido. The things about me that made me gay were the things about me that made me Italian-American. As a teenager, I paid close attention to my hair, fussed over my clothing, and had an eccentric knowledge of Renaissance artists and operatic plot. This might have pegged me as queer to my peers, except for one thing: my ethnicity. It was simply expected of an Italian-American. Growing up, there was never any reason to separate my gay side from my Italian-American side; they were almost one and the same. Upon coming out, guido became gay guido, without much of a noticeable difference.

Far from its macho reputation, Italy has one of the world's gayest cultures. Art, opera, fashion, and the long running drag show called the Catholic Church all come from there. So, in spite of our ethnic love of drama, I never understand when there is uproar over anything openly gay in Italy. When I heard about the first World Pride, held in Rome in the year 2000, it became a tipping point for me to plan an extended trip to the homeland. I had already wanted to go for the Millennium Jubilee to see the events that the Catholic Church had planned for *Il Giubileo*, the 2,000-year anniversary of the birth of Christ. Within the United States, many of my old relatives were dying off—including my beloved Aunt RoseAnn who tried to teach us old Italian and Catholic traditions (though I am not actually Catholic)—so I wanted to visit Italy to see where we traced our roots before I lost anymore. These forces—family, Catholicism, and homosexuality, which are seemingly at odds with each other, all of

92

which stare at you in the face when looking at Italy through the ages—were why I decided to make my year 2000 pilgrimage.

Although the Pope had tried to destroy World Pride, the idea of seeing such a leader enthralled me. During my first week in Rome, I signed up to be a part of the public audience for the Pope, so that I could see him in St. Peter's. It was hard to believe that this little man, who was so unassuming out of his church drag, could have so much power. Still, my heart fluttered the moment that he passed five feet from me, in an open air version of his Pope mobile, with men who looked like *mafiosos* at his side, and Cardinals wearing hot pink zucchettos, in the seats behind him. I waited for him to pass by me, and my camera was ready. I was alone, except for the Swiss Guards who surrounded me, aloof and handsome, dressed in their harlequin patterned leggings, tightly clinging to their muscular thighs.

I never lost my gay side at the Vatican. I spoke with the press about being gay, I cruised other men, and in the Sistine Chapel, under the famous outstretched hands of flaming sodomite Michelangelo's God and Adam, I made my own heavenly connection. I have the Pope to thank for that.

It was exciting to watch the World Pride events grow as the week continued. At first, Pride Park, which was located on one of the ancient seven hills that overlooked the city, consisted of a few tents for vendors. Eventually, Pride Park became "the" popular gay place in Rome, with thousands shopping, drinking, and socializing, as ancient ruins were lit to represent the colors of the Gay Pride Rainbow Flag.

Throughout the week, I also connected with many friends from New York. Interestingly, not a single one of them was Italian-American. However, none of that mattered. When the day of the actual parade came, we New Yorkers made our way to the Piramide Metro Station in Rome, where tens of thousands had gathered. Music blared from floats, drag queens posed and primped, rainbow balloons and flags fluttered overhead, and gorgeous men ran around in gladiator outfits. The overall scene was like that of any Pride Parade, except that we waited in the shadows of a Roman fortress, and the gladiators took us back thousands of years.

Rome's LGBT community had proven to the world that they could pull this off, in spite of the obstacles from both the Church and the State. For me, there will never be another Gay Pride celebration that will feel as special as World Pride 2000, and one that combined my own seemingly contradictory identities.

However, during that week, homophobia still persisted in Rome. On a stroll with friends who held hands, someone shouted in Italian, "Where's my gun?" On a train to the beach in Ostia, a Catholic pilgrim tried to talk to us about changing our sinful ways. In challenging her, I quoted from the Bible, and then she pretended to no longer understand English.

But none of this overshadowed the wonders that I saw as I traveled throughout Italy. In Pompeii, a gay couple held hands and kissed as comfortably as on Christopher Street. In Naples, two young lesbians held hands at the train station, amidst stares from the more conservative folks. Even alone, I made a statement by holding my rainbow water bottle holder while some Italians noticed. Many of them looked, pointed, and whispered among themselves, which made me realize that the Gay Pride events in Rome made them aware of this international gay symbol.

At the dawn of the first millennium, when Christians were persecuted and thrown to the lions for entertainment in this imperial capital, no one would have expected Rome to become the Catholic center of the world. And now that we are in the third millennium, Rome is becoming a new gay destination, despite its homophobia.

And this gay guido was proud to have been a part of it.

ADOPTED SON

David Masello

My 84-year-old father's best friend is a man younger than me. For many months, I've heard about Billy: how he knocks on the door of my father's second-floor unit at 11 o'clock at night, accompanied by his pug, Sylvester. Almost every night, Billy comes into my father's apartment. He unfolds the lawn chair that leans against a corner, while my father sits in the recliner, with his crossword puzzle book on his lap. They talk about military history, especially the Civil War and World War I.

"The kid knows his battle campaigns," my father says. "And the dog is cute as hell. But I'm always wary that it's going to have an accident on the carpet. So we never stay long in the apartment. I make up some excuse to go outside and sit by the pool where I can smoke. And so that's where we usually end up. We stay there sometimes until one, two in the morning. He's a great kid. Old people down here don't interest me a bit."

My father has taken to referring to Billy as his adopted son, and he uses this expression often in his presence. "The funny thing is he reminds me of you," my father says. "He looks like you. 'Wait 'till you meet my son in New York, you could be brothers,' I tell him. The moment I met him, I liked him because of the resemblance. I joke with him that he's got to be an Italian kid deep down."

While I am grateful that my father has a friend in his complex, I've always remained suspicious of Billy. After all, why would a married, 30-something-year-old want to spend so much time with my near-deaf father, talking about troop strategies at Gettysburg and

Verdun, and later drive to an all-night donut shop in a bad neighborhood of St. Petersburg.

My father's complex is filled with questionable residents, most of whom work jobs as Target assistant managers or waitpersons at Applebee's; telemarketers are regarded as elite professionals. Like arrestees in an episode of *Cops*, an inordinate number of the men walk around bare-chested, while the women schlep along holding the hands of children who are so young that I can't tell if they are sisters of the kids, or the mothers. Eviction notices from the U.S. Marshall are taped to a few doors, and some of the battered cars in the lot are affixed with police boots.

When my father first moved to Shadow Run, it was a neat, working-class development filled with people who had come from the North to retire, or to start a new life. But later, a portion of the units were set aside by the county, as low-income housing, which was a change that I had never explained to my father, but was now making itself increasingly evident to him.

During one of my visits to my father's apartment, I tell him that I want to meet Billy and take him out to dinner to thank him for all the favors that he has done, especially the most recent one, in which he helped my father after his car broke down.

"I was out driving around, about 10 o'clock at night, and suddenly my car starts acting up," my father tells me. "The god-damned thing stalls on me, right in traffic on Starkey Road. I'm able to coast near to the shoulder, but I don't make it all the way, and then that's it, it's dead. What a world we live in. Rather than someone getting out of their car to help me, which is what you would have expected in my day, everyone starts honking, giving me the finger. And you can imagine the kinds of things they're saying out their windows as they go around me. It's a good thing I don't hear well; otherwise, I'd teach some of them a lesson. I'm still capable of that, you know. So, guess who should show up within a few minutes? Billy. He's like some sort of guardian angel for me. He's always there when you need him. Like you."

Then, I hear about how Billy happened to be driving down the same road at that moment. Billy pulled over, pushed my father's car to the shoulder, and called for a tow truck on his cell phone. Then, he went with my father to the garage and waited for two hours as they fixed the car. Afterwards, he followed my father home.

"I just don't understand," I say. "How was it that Billy just happened to be driving along the same road at that moment?" I've heard versions of this story many times.

"He just was," my father says with irritation. "He knows my routine, how I like to take drives at night, smoke in the car, and go for a donut." He pauses. "I'm always complaining about this generation, how they're nothing compared to my generation. But then I think of Billy. And my three sons, of course. You're the exceptions. Down here, you see a lot of trash."

Before our dinner at the Olive Garden, my father tells me that Billy comes from Maine and that his father walked out on the family when Billy was a boy. "I think the kid never got over it and he thinks of me as, well, you can imagine, some kind of father figure, or whatever the hell you'd call it. All I know is that every time we're together, Billy mentions that incident and how he hates his father for it. I'm not even sure if he knows the father is alive or dead. Can you imagine that? When I think of my sweet dad, when your mother and I would visit him in Jersey, and we would drive away, he'd start to weep. I remember one time when we drove off, but left something at the house and had to go back. Oh, the scene he made when we returned, sobbing all over again, dropping the wet bread from his hand that he was feeding to the birds. Ah, it breaks my heart to think about it."

When I meet Billy, I'm surprised that my father is right. He does resemble me: tall, glasses, brown hair, although he's a much bigger version.

On the short drive to the restaurant, Billy sits in the back and my father is in the passenger seat. After I ask him how long he's been living in Florida, Billy says, "I came down from Maine after college, seventeen years ago. I wanted as big a change as you could find. When I was a boy, thirteen, my father dumped me and my mom and my brothers and sisters; there are seven of us. I've been processing that all my life. It's something you don't forget. You're lucky to have a dad like Mario here."

I note that he calls my dad by his given name rather than the name Tom that he *adopted* during his service in World War II.

Billy is personable and genuinely inquisitive about my life in New York. "Your dad tells me everything about you and your brothers," he says, proving it by reiterating recent professional developments and details about my life: how I pace my roof at night; the price of my small one-bedroom apartment; how I sometimes have lunch at Grand Central Station's Oyster Bar, a place my father worked as a cashier in the late 1930s, and where he was on a first-name basis with one of his regulars, Eddie Rickenbacker, the famous World War I ace. Billy mentions nothing about my romantic life, for which I am grateful.

"And he tells me everything about you," I say. "How much you do for him, your job with computers, the dog, and the talks you have. He's crazy about you. This dinner, by the way, is just a token of thanks for all you do. So please, order anything you want."

At the table, as I talk, my father retreats to eating since he's not able to hear what we're saying above the din of the restaurant.

"I wish I could be treating you and your wife to this dinner," I say. "You both deserve it."

"Well, I really like your dad. My visits with him are not a duty or anything like that. We have some good times together." Then says to my father, "Right, Mario?"

"What?" my father says, sipping a glass of rosé, so sweet that it makes him wince.

"I was telling your son here how much I enjoy our talks in the evening. How I look forward to them."

"You're a great kid, Billy," my father says. "Did I tell you I call him my favorite adopted son?" my father says to me. "I don't know what I'd do without you, Billy boy."

After my father says this, he rubs my neck in affection, but I wish he had instead reached across the table to touch Billy, who looks at my father's kneading hand and then down at his plate.

After Billy finishes his first bite of ravioli, he says to me, "I was fourteen when I found the Lord and He changed my whole attitude. I was getting out of control at that point, you know, with no father around. I was getting into trouble. My sisters prayed for me. My mother prayed for me. And their prayers were answered. How old were you when the Lord came into your life?"

These remarks, I realized, were the price of having Billy in my father's life. And when I heard them, they disoriented me, even frightened me a little because such rhetoric is so unfamiliar where I live, in Manhattan. But I was determined not to register any surprise. I considered whether these were the words of someone unbalanced and with an agenda for helping my father, or the not-so-uncommon remarks you hear in the working-class inland Florida landscapes. In trying to disguise my discomfort with his question, I say, "Well, I guess I'm too much of an urban guy. But anyone who believes the way you do is fortunate."

At the end of dinner, I tell my father to wait by the entrance while Billy and I retrieve the car. My father holds a Styrofoam carton containing a quarter of a breast of chicken parmigiana, a tube of garlic bread, and a handful of sugar packets that he threw in as we got up from the table; everyone leaving the restaurant lumbers along carrying at least one such carton. As we walk to the car, Billy says, "With my grandfather, I remember he was 84, the age when everything started to go wrong. Up to then, he was fine and active, like Mario. But I see your dad starting to slow down, as I'm sure you do."

Of course I knew my father was overdue for some medical woe, but couldn't imagine how he or I would manage it. "Some day, I know, I'm going to get one of those middle-of-the-night calls."

"Don't get me wrong," Billy says, "I didn't mean to sound like something out of Luke or Paul about gloom and doom and all. It's just that everyone needs to be ready for such developments. If anything does happen to your dad, I'll be around to help out, so don't worry. These things happen suddenly, and you've got to make adjustments."

Back at his complex, my father suggests we three sit around the pool. Billy says that he wants to go to his unit, first, though, to get his saxophone, so that he can play a tune for us. He returns with a gleaming soprano saxophone, its golden bore madly reflecting the spotlit pool water. His panting dog waddles beside him. As soon as I drag plastic chairs to a table, my father begins his pipe ritual: a flip of the tobacco pouch, dipping of a white felt cleaner into the stem, careful packing and tamping of the bowl. After several attempts at lighting humid-moist matches, accompanied by curses about Florida, my father's pipe bowl glows orange, above which a smear of gnats hovers.

Billy then starts to play one of my father's always-requested songs, *The Roses of Piccardy*, a World War I favorite. "Oh, I love this one," my father says as soon as he discerns the tune. "Please, one favor, when my time comes, play this at my you-know-what. Sometimes I think I was reincarnated on Flanders Fields."

When Billy finishes, my father says, "My son here used to play the piano. Like a pro, like Liberace. The number of years I've been asking him to sit down and play that tune. But he won't."

"I can't," I say. "I haven't played the piano in twenty years."

"Nonsense," my father says. "You don't lose a talent like that."

I want my father to compliment Billy on his playing, but the closest he gets to saying anything is, "Billy, I'm glad you could join us tonight. And sometime, when your wife isn't working the late shift, I'd like us all to go out together. I rarely get to see Dawn; she's a pretty girl."

My father puts his hand over my left arm, which rests on the table. "Who'd of guessed during my years in this god forsaken state of Florida that I'd be sitting in a place like this with my baby son on one side and my new adopted son on the other. Life is funny, especially at my age."

"So, *é ch'accade*," Billy says suddenly.

My father laughs.

"That's *your* expression," I say to my father.

"You're right," Billy says. "But I'm so used to hearing it that I say it for him now. I think it translates something like, 'It's what happens.'"

After a while, my father says that he needs to go to the apartment to use the bathroom. "But you two stay here," he insists. "I'll be back."

When my father doesn't return after a half hour, I tell Billy I'll go check on him. I find my father working the crossword puzzle, with The Weather Channel on, a map of Pennsylvania sliding across the screen.

"I thought you were coming back," I say to him.

"I can't take the heat. Plus, I figured you and Billy could talk."

"Billy's still by the pool. He's expecting us again."

"I'm too tired, to be honest. Stay here with me and visit awhile."

"But what about Billy?"

"He'll wait for us. You can count on him. Stay here for 15 minutes and go back to him."

But as my father continues to scrawl on the crossword puzzle grid, I drift off to sleep and awake 45 minutes later, to an episode of *The Golden Girls.*

"You shouldn't have let me sleep," I tell my father.

"I drifted off, too."

"I wonder if Billy is still waiting for us."

"What do you mean?" my father asks.

"Billy. I told him to wait by the pool for me to come back."

"He's probably with the dog," my father says. "I wouldn't worry about him."

I return to the pool as quickly as I can. Billy is still at the table, his dog in his lap.

"Everything okay?" he asks.

"Yeah. Fine. I'm sorry. My father fell asleep, and I'm afraid I did, too. You didn't have to wait."

"Mario coming back for more visiting?"

"I think he's a bit tired."

"I guess he wants to spend some time alone with you," Billy says. "He couldn't wait for you to arrive. He's been talking about it all week."

Billy gets up from the chair, puts his dog on the ground, and secures the leash. He slings the saxophone over a shoulder.

"Well, I'll be seeing you later in the week, I hope," Billy says. "If not, I certainly understand. You and your dad will be spending time together doing all of the sightseeing he says you like to do. He always says he loves it when his sons visit, but hates it when they leave. He says the minute you arrive, he starts dreading the moment you'll have to leave. Mario and I will resume our nightly routine after you're gone."

"I'm sure he'll welcome that."

"It'll help. But I know it can't compare to one of your visits. How could it?"

I return to the apartment and find my father ready to go out, pipe and donut coupons in hand. "How about going out for a donut and coffee before you head back to the motel?" he asks. "It'll give us more time to be together."

A year later, when I did receive that middle-of-the-night call about my father, Billy was the one to whom I sent a key to my father's apartment, bequeathing him my father's flea-market furniture and supermarket artwork. In the course of the clean-up, the actual and the emotional, Billy called one day to tell me that the so-called supervisor of the apartment complex had broken into my father's apartment and had taken the keys to my father's car. Neither Billy nor I could control the demise of my father or the people and events taking advantage of him.

Once my father's affairs were settled, Billy wrote to tell me that he was getting a divorce and would most likely be moving to Texas or Arizona, or one of those Sunbelt states that beckon to un-rooted Americans. In the several years since, I have never been able to find Billy, a man who, for a short while, occupied the place of a son and brother in our family.

"MA TU SEI PAZZO?!"
NOTES FROM A RADICAL SOUTHERN ITALIAN/AMERICAN QUEER ACTIVIST

Tommi Avicolli Mecca

Whenever she had an audience, Mamma would sometimes tell the story of how she believed I got my start as a queer activist. She was proud of what I had done, and gave it that old southern Italian flair, meaning lots of dramatic inflections in her voice and, of course, her hands dancing wildly as if they were doing an aerial tarantella.

The story takes place in Catholic school in the heart of South Philly where I was born and raised. It was the early 60s and the Immaculate Heart of Mary nuns ran our local school like a blue-robed Gestapo. Repressed is an understatement. Their concept of morality was firmly entrenched in the Middle Ages.

One particular nun spent a lot of time gossiping about the people, particularly those of Italian extraction, who lived in the neighborhood. I don't remember her name or what grade I was in (fourth or fifth, I believe). But she should have been teaching us about geography or history. Basically, she trashed those folks, particularly this one poor soul, a widower, who never went to Sunday Mass, but instead stayed home to stir his tomato sauce, she claimed. God didn't take kindly to the slight, and eventually burned down the widower's house, which then prompted an editorial about how horrible, and what lousy Catholics, Italians were.

One day, as Mamma told it, I stood up and shouted, "Basta!" If Puccini were directing it, I would have gone into a very loud and intense aria. Although I vaguely remember what I said, Mamma's version had me reading that nun the Declaration of Guinea Rights.

Incidentally, that was the same nun who told my mother at the annual open house that I draped my sweater over my shoulders like a girl, in front of a line of other parents and kids standing behind us. She once admonished me for staring at a boy in class: "someone might get the wrong idea," she cautioned.

Note to Sister: the wrong idea was the right idea.

TESTA DURA

I think it was actually Mamma who inspired me to become an activist.

We were dirt poor during those first 10 or so years of my life. Then we moved on up to the working-class. Papa ran a gas station with his brother, my Uncle Jack. They managed to eke out a modest living. For Uncle Jack, the money stretched further because he and his wife had no kids. For Papa, there were four young mouths to feed. And sometimes there were more mouths to feed when my Nonno, and my Mamma's sister, my godmother, whom I suspect was a friend of Dorothy's, lived with us.

In order to make ends meet, Mamma aggressively haggled with the neighborhood merchants. A little bit off here, a little bit off there. Every tiny savings helped her put food on the table with the small allowance Papa gave her.

Mamma was a spitfire. Her family was from Avigliano in the region of Basilicata in southern Italy where the people were reputed to be stubborn and strong-willed, full of testa dura. She fought with everyone, especially Papa's famiglia, which hailed from Monteroduni in the region of Molise. Papa's sisters had married men who made enough dough to move them into Upper Darby, a suburb of

Philly. They weren't rich, but they enjoyed middle-class life, 60's-style. They even had a real garden in the back with the most incredible rose bushes. My garden was a rectangular cinderblock enclosure that Papa constructed and filled with dirt from the dumps on the outskirts of the city.

Papa's sisters wouldn't even come to our house; it was beneath them, which made Mamma livid. She spent her life trying to prove to them, and to herself, that she was just as good as they were.

She also also fought with the local clergy. One year, when the priest arrived at the door for the "Annual Visitation," she greeted him with a string of southern Italian expletives. He had come for a donation, 10% of Papa's income was the suggested amount, but she didn't have that much to give. She said she had it "up to here" with our name appearing at the bottom of the list of contributors, from highest to lowest, that the church published in the monthly bulletin that it sent to all the parishioners.

Years later, in a final act of defiance, she refused last rites from my cousin, the priest, when she lay dying.

SEXUAL AWAKENING

By the time I was 16, I was an avowed atheist and had come to doubt all that I was being taught in Catholic school. I was sneaking off to civil rights and anti-Vietnam War demos. My descent into skepticism started with a brush with gay sex in a dark alley one summer night after a neighborhood boy and I stole a copy of *Playboy* from the local drugstore. We were bored. He suddenly decided he simply had to see those big-breasted, pink-fleshed women that the magazine splattered all over its shiny pages.

I could've cared less about those women, but he was another matter altogether. I had been drawn to boys since I was about five. I used to stare at the olive-skinned boy next door from a hole in the yard fence. Even at that young age, the sight of him aroused a feeling in me I couldn't comprehend. It also set a pattern for the rest of my life: I still drool at the sight of black hair and olive skin.

It was easy enough to get *Playboy* out of the store without being seen. Kids got lots of five-finger discounts there, usually candy. My friend was ecstatic. As he hungrily paged through the magazine, he began to grope himself. Then he asked me to get down on my knees.

It was no secret that I was queerly disposed. I jumped rope with the girls in the neighborhood. I was sometimes seen out on the stoop with my sister playing with her dolls. It didn't take a rocket scientist to figure out what I was. Kids in the neighborhood and at school had names for me. They all stung.

I couldn't sleep that night. I knew God was going to strike me down for what I had done. It was a mortal sin of the absolute worst kind. I said my Act of Contrition several times. It didn't help. I could sense that God was gunning for me. He was going to make me suffer the most agonizing death possible, like those poor slobs who burned to death in Sodom and Gomorrah.

When I woke the next morning to another beautiful hot summer day, I felt a crack in the wall of fear, which the nuns instilled in me. I didn't become an atheist right away, but the seed that was planted that morning grew to full maturation by the time I was 16 and I was reading those subversive queer writers: Jean Genet and Allen Ginsberg.

One day I simply decided that God belonged in the same discard pile as Santa Claus and the Tooth Fairy. I was content to be "condemned to freedom," as Sartre put it. Then I met someone, and I fell madly and irrationally in love. He was an olive-skinned, black-haired Sicilian boy—no surprise there. Sartre would have approved.

GAY LIBERATION

Two years of an "affair" with that classmate ended rather abruptly a couple of nights before Halloween in 1969, when he suddenly told me he didn't want to see me again. I still don't know why. I'm guessing that our relationship had gotten too intense for him. Since the night we first met, we had been joined at the hip. We had even decided to go to the same college and live on campus together.

I wanted to die. I contemplated ending it all with a razor blade, but not knowing what I was actually doing combined with a fear of facing the unknown kept me from harming myself.

Luckily, I had just started classes at Temple University in North Philly. That first semester I discovered two amazing organizations that helped me forget that boy: the campus chapter of SDS (Students for a Democratic Society, an anti-Vietnam group) and the Gay Liberation Front (GLF). I didn't feel much affinity for school, so I spent a lot of time being an activist rather than a student. I was only in college to avoid the draft. I was too cowardly to do what friends had done: walk into the neighborhood recruitment office and declare that I was queer. I knew instinctively that the news would spread throughout the streets of Little Italy within seconds of the words leaving my lips.

After I walked into a GLF meeting on one Friday afternoon, gay liberation became my obsession. Within weeks of joining the group, I was elected "chairperson." We only appointed leaders because, as an official student organization that received funding from the University (how we pulled that off is another story altogether), we were required to present the Office of Student Affairs with a list of officers and a copy of our constitution. I was basically the person who had to answer for anything controversial we did. And we managed to do a lot of controversial things during my time there.

One of our controversial things was opposing Aversion (or "Shock") Therapy. The school's counseling department was routinely referring gay men to the Eastern Pennsylvania Psychiatric Institute (EPPI), where they were subjected to a form of "therapy" in which they were shown slides of cute naked guys and then jolted with electricity through electrodes attached to their dicks. It was supposed to "shock" them into heterosexuality.

It didn't work, of course, but regardless, it was a barbaric practice and we pledged to stop it. We eventually succeeded! Our campaign got the attention of a very popular late-night talk show host.

Big trouble was brewing.

PUCCINI WOULD HAVE HAD A FIELD DAY

When the talk show representative called and asked if one of us would debate a shrink from EPPI, everyone pointed to me. I was doing most of the grunt work on the campaign, anyway. I reluctantly agreed.

Ma tu sei pazzo? (Are you nuts?) I asked myself several times as I headed home that afternoon. How could I appear on TV when *la mia famiglia* didn't know I was queer, let alone a big gay activist on campus?

Nonetheless, I went to the taping. I was so fired up with a new-found gay militancy that nothing could have kept me away. I was so obnoxious during the program that I wouldn't let the rep from EPPI get a word in edgewise. At one point the director held up a card telling the host to "shut him up." It didn't work.

I told Mamma the day before the program aired. She was hysterical, not only because I was gay, but because Papa would find out. No one wanted to deal with the raging bull. When he went on a tirade, we all ducked for cover. Usually a gentle soul, Papa got out of control when faced with something that challenged his conservative political beliefs, like the sight of hippies or antiwar demonstrators on TV, or the Beatles on Ed Sullivan.

I disobeyed Mamma. I didn't tell Papa before the show aired. I figured, he'll never see it, he goes to bed early, the program airs at 1 a.m. Papa didn't see it. My uncle, the cop, did. And he called Papa to let him know that his youngest son was a finuck (from "finocchio," fennel, southern Italian slang for fag).

All hell broke loose in my house. Papa went on a tirade. I had never seen him so angry. My godfather, Uncle Johnny, called to say that he was never talking to me again. He never did. In fact, when my father died, he snubbed me at the wake -- and that was 17 years after I came out. Another uncle suggested to my oldest brother that they take care of me, *Godfather* style. My mother's family, on the other hand, continued to treat me as if I had not "shamed the family," as Papa's kin charged.

When the dust settled, I was banished from la mia casa and Papa didn't talk to me for about 15 years. Mamma remained in touch with me, stopping in at work to see me. She became my staunchest supporter, defending me to family members and neighbors alike. My godmother, Mamma's sister, the unmarried one, who used to live with us, also visited me at my job to make sure I had enough to eat. My siblings were fine, too; they rolled with the punches that they were no doubt receiving from Papa's family.

My oldest brother ultimately performed a miracle: he got Papa to agree that I could come along when he and his girlfriend visited for Xmas one year. It was a strange reunion. Papa didn't say much. He asked if I had enough money, and, as we were taking off, he offered me an old coat. "That one you're wearing's not warm enough," he said. It was. He just didn't like the style of the jacket. The one he gave me was far too conservative for me to be seen in.

But I accepted the olive branch, tears flooding my eyes. We had finally made peace.

A few weeks later, Papa was dead.

Puccini would have had a field day with my life.

GIVING VOICE

I beat him to it. In 1985, I decided to put my own life on stage. I was a well-known queer activist in Philly. I wrote for the *Philadelphia Gay News* and other publications. But I had a lot of demons with which to contend.

Confessional art was all the rage. So I wrote *Giving Voice*, a performance art piece that utilized dance, song, poetry, and prose to tell the story of a sissy growing up in South Philly's Little Italy, an effeminate boy who still bore the scars of having been tormented and made to feel that he was the problem when clearly his bullies were. It was cathartic, to say the least.

It wasn't just about being gay; *Giving Voice* was ultimately a celebration of being a queer Italian/American man. As such, it was, as far as I know, the first of its kind. At a time when most Italian/American queers were still content to remain in their closets, I was going where no wop had gone before.

Giving Voice received rave reviews and played to sold-out audiences, which was a complete shock to me. The work was so personal that I had no idea people would love it so much. When *paesani* from South Philly came up to me and told me I made them cry, I knew I had succeeded.

Images of a War Unfought was my next theatrical work. It took *Giving Voice* to another level. It focused on a gay man with AIDS, who holds two college jocks hostage for being his former neighborhood tormenters. It was the ultimate revenge fantasy. *The Philadelphia Inquirer* critic got it right; he found it provocative and "wish fulfillment." At the end of the play, as lights blacked out, the gay man shot one of the jocks who refused to repent for his bullying.

The 80s were a dark decade. As more and more friends died of AIDS, the anger in me grew and grew. I was tagged the "angry performance artist" by a national arts magazine. I founded Avalanche, a multi-racial queer theatre troupe collective that did cutting edge material about our queer lives. We struck a nerve. All of our shows were sold out.

In the 80s, my Italian politics became more radical. I read about the history of southern Italy, how after Rome fell, the land of my ancestors was conquered by so many different countries. I also learned about the discrimination Italians faced when they emigrated here: NINA (No Italian Need Apply) signs in shop windows, lynchings in the south, and negative stereotypes in movies and on TV.

I wrote a piece for the *South Philadelphia Review Chronicle*, the neighborhood paper serving the Italian/American community, calling on Italians to reject Columbus and, instead, celebrate the legacy of Sacco and Vanzetti, two anarchists from southern Italy who fought for the rights of workers. They were falsely accused of murder, I believe, and executed by the state of Massachusetts in 1924, despite international cries to spare them.

It was like yelling "dago" in a crowded Italian restaurant.

HEY PAESAN

I moved to San Francisco in October of 1991. Too many friends had died. Philly felt like a graveyard. The realization that I desperately needed a change came when, at an exhibition of the AIDS quilt, I broke down in tears as I was reading a list of names of those who had died. I just couldn't stop crying that night.

Before I left, I penned a memoir for *Philadelphia Magazine*, entitled "Memoirs of a South Philly Sissy," which received tons of responses, including many from young Italian/American queers thanking me for my courage in being so out of the closet. I didn't see most of those letters; I heard about them from my editor, Lisa DePaulo, after I moved.

Lisa and I became friends during the Anthony Milano murder trial in 1987. An Italian immigrant who was a closeted gay man, Milano had his throat slashed by two homophobic guys in Bucks County, outside of Philly. I was covering the trial for the *Philadelphia Gay News*, Lisa for *Philadelphia Magazine*. Neither of us were prepared for the horrific details of the murder that would emerge during the weeks of the trial. I had very vivid nightmares and couldn't sleep. The sight of his sweet Italian parents, so frail and frightened, was too much. Every day, I fought to keep from sobbing in the courtroom.

My first contact with the Bay Area's Italian/American community was in 1992 when thousands took to the street to protest the quincentenary of Columbus' arrival on the shores of the "new world." I joined the "Italians against Columbus" contingent.

In the next few years, I would meet two amazing Italian/American lesbians, Giovanna Capone and Denise Nico Leto, and we would edit the first anthology of Italian/American queer writing, *Hey Paesan!: Writings by Lesbians and Gay Men of Italian Descent*, and inspire Anthony Julian Tamburri of Bordighera Press to publish *Fuori: Essays by Italian/American Lesbians and Gays*, a smaller version of our anthology. We co-founded the annual "Dumping Columbus" poetry and prose reading that had its kickoff at a cabaret owned by an Italian gay man and now occurs at City Lights Bookstore in the North Beach area of the city, once a solidly Italian/Sicilian neighborhood.

A HALLOWEEN BLOWJOB

There was other work, too. I found a great and affordable place in the Castro two days after I arrived. You could do that in those days. I got a job on Castro Street at A Different Light Bookstore, then a three-store gay bookstore chain owned by two gay men. Life in the Castro was wild and wonderful. It was bouncing back from the devastation that the neighborhood had suffered during the 80s AIDS crisis.

On weekends, the corner of 18th & Castro was hopping with political activity. Activists set up ironing boards with literature or stood with petitions in hand. There was always a gathering in Harvey Milk Plaza to protest something. On Halloween, it was like a coming together of the many tribes that made up our community.

During my first Halloween in the Castro, I met a group of Radical Faeries one block from the bookstore. We stripped down, painted each other's bodies, and then marched through the crowd to 18th & Castro where we formed a circle. At some point, someone grabbed my dick and then went down on me, right there in the middle of the street, as some people in the crowd applauded. I felt as if I had reached the Emerald City.

The feeling was short-lived. When the dot-com boom hit in the late 90s like a tsunami, sending rents through the sky, many young queers, fleeing to The Castro as they have since the 60s, found themselves unable to afford an apartment. They started lining the Castro asking for change and sleeping in the doorways of shops. Many merchants and neighbors went ballistic.

The Rev. Jim Mitulski, then minister of the Metropolitan Community Church, and I organized three winter shelters, a free meals program, and a place to get a shower.

The other negative effect of the boom was that greed became epidemic among landlords. Desperate to rent to the dot-com workers who preferred to live in San Francisco rather than Silicon Valley to the south, they used every trick in the book (some legal, some not) to get long-term tenants, who were protected by rent control, out of their apartments, so they could re-rent them for more money.

In the Castro, scores of gay men with AIDS, who were long-term tenants, who had been in their places since the early 70s, were pushed out. Talk about class warfare. While the mainstream AIDS organizations stood by and did nothing, a group of us organized protests against the realtors and landlords doing the evictions.

Unfortunately, we lost the battle. Today, the Castro is upscale, not completely queer, and unwelcoming to poor and homeless folks. There's no more Halloween celebration, no more weekly activist tables at 18th & Castro, and far fewer protests at Harvey Milk Plaza. Queer organizations don't rent office space above the stores; it's far too expensive.

Instead of "ACT UP, fight back," people typically wear "Abercrombie and Fitch" tee-shirts. It feels like history is repeating itself.

PRICE OF THE TICKET

A hundred years ago, Italian/Sicilian radicals mobilized in much the same way that queers did in the Gay Liberation Movement of the early 70s, or in ACT UP in the late 80s. These *sovversivi*, as they were called, were active in all of the major labor strikes. They helped organize workers, such as those in the garment industry in New York. They had an analysis of oppression and class, setting up discussion groups and publishing newspapers in Italian to spread the word about their revolutionary ideas. They understood that this country to which they had come was not a land of the free. There were no streets paved with gold, but instead with the blood, sweat, and tears of immigrants and other workers. Speaking out meant being persecuted, executed, or deported, but they were brave and kept up the fight even when the odds were against them.

Their names are mostly forgotten, but we need to remember them: Carlo Tresca, Arturo Giovannitti, Luigi Galleani, Maria Roda, Angela Bambace, Mary Nardini, Bellalma Forzato-Spezia, and Virgilia D'Andrea, among so many thousands of others.

There was Camella Teoli, a girl barely in her teens when she had the top part of her head cut off after her hair became tangled in a machine she operated in a textile mill in Massachusetts. At 14, she testified before Congress about her experiences as a child laborer.

There was the New York's most progressive Congressman, Vito Marcantonio, a member of the American Labor Party, who championed black civil rights in the 30s and 40s, and pushed for federal anti-lynching laws. He formed a coalition between Puerto Ricans and Italians living in East Harlem, which was the center of his district.

In the queer community we have an incredible history of resistance as well. On four occasions that we know of, street queens and hustlers, many of them of color, all of them people at the bottom of the totem pole in the queer and straight communities, rose up to say "No!" to the unrelenting homophobia and transphobia with which they lived every day of their lives: Cooper's Donuts in Los Angeles in 1959, Dewey's restaurant in Philadelphia in 1965, Compton's Cafeteria in San Francisco in 1966, and the Stonewall Inn in New York City in 1969.

After Stonewall, radical queers from many other left groups, such anti-war and civil rights, came fleeing out of their closets to form the most progressive LGBT movement ever to emerge in this country.

Now that gay marriage is becoming a household word, and gays and lesbians can serve in the military, not to mention be elected to

116

public office, and selected as a spokes-lesbian for major corporations, such as J.C. Penney, it's beginning to feel like that moment in Italian/American history when the *sovversivi* faded into the background and the desire to assimilate took center stage.

Will forgetting our radical roots be the price of the ticket to acceptance for the LBGT community as well?

If history repeats itself, it probably will be.

THE PROBLEM WITH ME IS...

Joe Oppedisano

I bet if you ask any Italian American man—gay, straight, bi, whatever—what his biggest fault is, he would say that it is his neurotic behavior brought on by none other than his family. And yes, the church also plays a major part in the demise of our souls, but it pales in comparison to the overbearing attention, love, and coddling we received as young boys.

Before I was born, my mother had eight miscarriages, which was why I was spoiled rotten. Not only did my mother worship, adore, and praise me every second of every day, she made me believe that the entire world would be the same way towards me. I was perfect. I was chosen. I was great. Then you realize the truth. Then you realize that not only are you not the center of the universe, but, in fact, you are below average, and on a scale of one to ten, you are maybe a four.

My mother would bake a loaf of bread every day for me, timing it to pop out of the oven, hot, fresh, and soaked in a stick of butter, just as I was walking down the steps from the school bus. But on the school bus, and all day at school, I was miserable, not understanding why all the other kids kept calling me a fat pig, a blimp, and a loser. Didn't they know that I was perfect? My mother told me so. It never crossed my mind that these underprivileged children who brought only a sandwich and a piece of fruit to lunch, really didn't like me. Of course they didn't, I was an obnoxious and overweight kid with wiry hair and a greasy forehead that seeped olive oil. But, I was also, as I was told by my mother, wonderful, funny, and important. So it didn't make sense that the other kids disliked me, and I would question it briefly as I devoured my loaf of bread while watching cartoons and having my head rubbed every afternoon by my mother. And every evening, after dinner, my mother told me to rest in bed, that my schoolwork could wait, and that I was too good to help with the dishes. She also told me that I was too important to mow the lawn, or do anything other chores around the house. "That's what your father's for," she told me. I was encouraged to be lazy.

She told me that everyone else was jealous of me, that they wanted to be me. That was the reason why I did not have any friends. I was always with adults, especially the women, usually in the kitchen. They told tales of the old country, even though none of them were actually born there. They spoke Italian dialect, and some English words were replaced by their Italian slang. They gossiped. They screamed. And we ate a lot.

The summer of my twelfth year, I lost thirty pounds in three months. Every morning, I played the Village People's "Macho Man" on my turntable while doing sit-ups and push-ups, and jogging in place for ten to twelve minutes until my head would get dizzy. I would fall down and breathe heavily, but I did it, and all by myself. It was hard, and my mother only made it worse. She thought that I was on the verge, and brought me to see my doctor, daily, because she was convinced that I had leukemia. She thought that I was going to die before her eyes, which was her worst fear. And as she cried every afternoon, in the car on the way to the doctor's office, she asked how and why God could do this to her. Day after day, the doctor would tell her that I didn't have leukemia, that I wasn't sick. But all she would do was cry and say, "He doesn't eat! He's so skinny! Why?"

Then one morning, at about 3 a.m., it all became perfectly clear. I was going through puberty. My mother was upset at me for putting

119

her through hell. She insisted that it was only a matter of time before I would leave her, one way or another, and that she would be crushed and probably die alone. Drama. Always.

After losing weight, I returned to school and my whole world changed. I noticed that girls checked me out. Guys said hello to me and told me to join them; we laughed and told jokes, teased the girls, and played games. Surprisingly, I was even invited to a birthday party. I was thrilled because I finally had friends. When I told my mother, she told me to get into the car, and we drove to the shopping mall to the men's store, and she bought me a suit for the party. It was tan, with shoulder pads, had a shine to it, like sharkskin, and when I moved in it, it caught the light and made me glisten. It was a trendy suit for that time.

My mother told me that I was handsome and that I would turn heads when I walked into the room. She told me that all of the other boys were jealous of me because I could be a model or movie star. So when I arrived at the party a week later, bearing gifts and sporting a corsage, which my mother bought and pinned on me right before she drove me to the party, I was not prepared for the catastrophe that was about to happen—and change me forever.

As I walked up the steps of the house, I felt good about myself. I thought that I looked so handsome; I felt so secure. I was excited to be part of this group of guys who stopped calling me "faggot" because of my new look. Then my friend's mom answered the door, wearing a kerchief, sunglasses, and a casual blouse. "Was I at the wrong address?" I thought. My mother noticed the women and honked the horn, for she, too, thought that I was at the wrong place. This woman was not in a gown; she was not possibly hosting a party. But she invited me in, and then asked me if I had just come from church. When I said no, she looked puzzled, and asked if I had brought my bathing suit because this was a pool party. And then as I looked past her, I noticed, that it was a co-ed party. I was not at all prepared to be seen half naked in front of guys, let alone girls. I panicked and started sweating. She walked me to the pool. The other kids stopped what they were doing, turned toward me, and giggled. I didn't want them to know that I was upset, so I went into the bathroom, locked the door behind me, and sat on the toilet. I was desperate for the time to fly by; I prayed for an earthquake, something, anything to get me out of this awkward party.

The mother came knocking, screaming for me to get out of the bathroom. I exclaimed that I had a bloody nose. So she banged even harder. "Open up!," she yelled back. When I finally opened the door, my heart sank again, as I saw all of the kids laughing and pointing at the crazy Italian boy, who was dressed in a suit on a ninety degree day, at a pool party. And when I looked up at the clock on the wall, my heart sank again because what had seemed like two hours in the bathroom only turned out to be ten minutes.

I called my mother, crying on the telephone, begging her to pick me up. She said no. She said that they would realize that they should look to me for advice on how to act and look because I was obviously more mature, handsome, talented, and wise. She told me that I was perfect. Obviously, this was not true. And this was my problem.

GROWING UP UN-ITALIAN-AMERICAN

Felice Picano

Since I permanently moved to Los Angeles, I've been assailed by casting agents. With my brown eyes, silver hair, and goatee, I was told that I could pass for many different ethnicities. I finally relented and signed with one talent agency. Infrequently, I go to print-ad and TV-commercial auditions. They usually call for a Hispanic man my age; it is, after all, southern California. I always fit in. Sometimes, the call is for a Middle-Eastern man, or a more generically "Mediterranean" man, and even for a Russian character. My agent assures me that I always look the part.

I recently went on my first audition calling for an Italian-American man.

The other men at the casting agency, who were waiting to audition before me, all looked really Italian, almost caricatures: big noses, big bodies. They had names, like Vito and Angelo and Mike. But hey, I'm Felice. And they were familiar, too, from smaller or bit parts in movies and TV shows that I'd seen, like *The Godfather, Part Twelve* and *The Sopranos.* They seemed to know each other, and they talked to each other in low voices. They never once spoke to me. They never brought me into their chats. I didn't stand a chance.

When I went in for my audition, the Italian-American interviewer took one look at me and told his assistant to call my agent and yell at her, explaining "I *distinctly* asked for Italian-Americans."

They knew! And even when I do look the look, and walk the walk, when it comes down to it, we are different. For an Italian-American, I am about as *Un*-Italian-American as you can get!

This used to come as a big surprise to me and always comes as a big surprise to other people who know me. My name is so Italian sounding. My father was born in Itri, southeast of Rome. He came to this country as an infant, and he wasn't "naturalized" as a U.S. citizen until he was 23 years old. When I was young, people told me that I resembled the movie star Sal Mineo. How Italian can you get?

I have been the victim of anti-Italian prejudice. Few were as overt as the time that I interviewed for a Woodrow Wilson Fellowship at Princeton University's Graduate School. While discussing Henry James' later novellas with one professor, I was rudely asked by another older professor, if wouldn't I be happier working in a barbershop? Several early reviews of my novels often had disguised attacks on my ethnicity. Years later, I realized that they were biased.

By now, I'm a fairly well-known author with two dozen books and four produced plays to my name. Yet, until a few years ago, I was never asked to be part of an Italian-American anything. Then, I was asked to contribute to an anthology called *Hey Paisan!: Writings by Lesbians and Gay Men of Italian Descent*, published in Oakland, California. My essay on my friend Nunzio D'Anarumo, from the 1960s and '70s, was published in the anthology; it was about how he and his siblings were haunted by their dead father in their upscale, suburban estate in Rhode Island. As I read the other essays in the book, it became clear to me that they were by gay men and women who were in constant and shocking rebellion against their Italian-American and Catholic families, which seemingly had no place for them or for their gay and lesbian lives. By contrast, I never asked to fit in, and never once considered what anyone else thought of me. Take me or leave me is my motto. And if you don't, it's your loss. So, once again, I didn't fit in.

I've never been asked to join an Italian-American writers' or artists' association, or to write for an Italian-American magazine, or raise money for an Italian-American charity, or political organization, or professional organization. Forget about the Knights of Columbus or any Columbus Day celebration. At least not until Michael and Joseph asked me into this collection. And here I'm going to stand out, too, which is okay with the editors, and which I'm used to by now.

᰽

Another problem for me is Roman Catholicism, which I'm not.

I guess in the beginning I was raised as a Roman Catholic. I have a photo of me in my parents' backyard on Long Island at age six, dressed for my First Communion, a requisite Catholic rite of passage. I look suitably angelic with my little white suit and white tie, holding a little missal.

So far, so good. Except, at age eleven, I came to a sudden and full consciousness as a person, in a way that I now think must have been similar to Saul's "conversion on the road to Damascus," with him ending up at St. Paul. Mine had quite different and not at all religious results, which I wrote about in my memoir, *Ambidextrous*. This meant that at eleven and a half and twelve, when young Catholics begin the process toward the next rite of passage, Confirmation (as a "Soldier of God," we were told, hup, hup, hup!), I was questioning everything anyone told me.

Everything!

Anyone!

After I had questioned a number of catechism facts taught in Friday afternoon, religious school Confirmation classes, which I found to be "historically unsound" and "geologically improbable," I was politely informed by Sister Mary William Whomever that I was a "disruptive element." I was asked not to return to class again.

Most of my friends in my sixth and seventh grade Advanced Placement classes were Jewish, and they were appalled by this reaction. They went to Friday afternoon religious school classes, too, in process toward their own pre-teen Confirmation rite, called Bar Mitzvah. So the following Friday, I went to the Synagogue (or *Schul*) along with them. I was welcomed. I was allowed, in fact, encouraged, to ask questions. This seemed more like it.

I attended many Passovers and Succoths and went around and received Chanukah "gelt" with my buddies, and I even helped a close friend learn his Hebrew well enough to give his little exegesis at his coming of age rite. I enjoyed another dozen or so pals' celebrations: food, dancing, gifts. What's *not* to like? But I never converted and I was never bar mitzvahed.

By then I had discovered history in some depth, going back to the Greeks, Egyptians, and Sumerians, and I came to understand that religion was kind of a relative thing. Eventually, during my twenties, I discovered Zen Buddhism, which struck me as more than enough religion for any intelligent person. I could fold my legs into a Lotus position; I could meditate. There weren't any messy rituals involved. Even better, there was no one to check up on me. This has led to some potentially embarrassing moments for others, not for me. For instance, the business meeting at which the speaker began, "Now, we're all Christians here!" So, I felt obliged to raise my hand to differ. Or, at my father's funeral where, to my utter astonishment, there was a Requiem Mass in a Roman Catholic Church.

I was allegedly the "lead mourner" for this exequy. After four decades, my memories of the Mass were dim at best. Even worse, it had all changed in those intervening decades: it was now spoken, not sung, and in English, not Latin, and the people in the congregation shook hands and they said things to each other, and handed around communion wafers like they were Saltine crackers. My Aunt Betty, my father's only living sister, came up with a solution: she sat behind me, telling me what to do, step by step: kneel, genuflect, stand up, etc. Thus, string puller and puppet, we avoided a complete disaster.

Another side of my Un-Italian-American-ness is when people are prejudiced towards me for not being Catholic. Most of the time, I simply don't understand the prejudice. Or if I do, I disconcert them by giving it back as good as I got it.

It's even worse when people with Irish, Polish, and Italian names try to place Catholic guilt trips on me if I don't do what they wish—and let's face it, I never do. Guilt and shame are utterly unknown to me, except as concepts in literature and psychology. So it's usually a day later that I recognize what they were trying on me, and then I burst out in laugher, often at inappropriate times, and in inappropriate places.

I've got nothing against Catholics, or for that matter with Italian-Americans. Just the opposite: a good Mass is terrific when done in a great Cathedral during a big holiday, Christmas Eve or Easter, with a half mile of flowers, and a quarter ton of rich hangings, and the soloists and choirs singing in Latin and not with a guitar. So, no wonder it all lasted as long as it did; that is high entertainment.

My Jewish lover always looked more Italian than I did. On Saturday afternoons, when my Jewish lover and I used to go around the Italian neighborhoods of Brooklyn that he (not I) knew well, for haircuts, pastry, produce, and meat, I used to feel very much at home. I loved the food, the language, the music, and the art. After all, I'd lived in Rome for months as a youth, and I would live in Florence in a minute if I could do so.

I watch Italian films. I read Italian authors. I love Pirandello's stories. And I go to Italian operas. I think of Italian men as one of my special "types": sexy, masculine, approachable, humorous, down to earth, and unique in their acceptance of their own identities and of other people's individualities. But it was clear that I was always a visitor, never a *paisan*. I never fit in. In Rome, I was always pegged as a foreigner. In Brooklyn, they were always surprised whenever I spoke Italian. And while I've learned to pepper it with "salty dialect" expressions, the truth is, even in Rome, they dubbed me *professorino* (little professor) because I spoke textbook, college-learned Italian, not street Italian.

But when I returned to my gay life in Manhattan, Fire Island, or Beverly Hills, I fit in perfectly. In those places, I feel at home.

❧

I blame my parents for feeling un-Italian-American, partly, because they're dead and I can blame them, at least without their rebuttal, but mostly because it was their various experiences and choices in life that are, after all, to blame for me being un-Italian-American.

Both of my parents grew up in Rhode Island, a state with a substantial Italian-American population, and many well-known Italian-American citizens. This includes several state governors and a chain of mayors of the city of Providence, a city that constitutes half the population and a quarter of the area of the entire state. Federal Hill is Providence's Italian-American neighborhood, and to this day, it is solidly Italian-American. Also, Rhode Island has its share of mobsters. And as for celebrities, Bernadette Peters comes to mind.

So why did my parents have to grow up in the sticks? In rural Thornton? It takes a minimum of twenty minutes by car to get to the closest Italian-American community inside the city of Cranston.

My father relocated to New York City to live with his Aunt Carrie and Uncle Sal Recco. There he completed his schooling, adolescence, and early manhood in the Ozone Park neighborhood of Queens, New York. During that time, the dominant ethnic groups in Ozone Park were Irish, German, and Jewish. Italian-Americans were the minority. My father recalled a great deal of animosity between the ethnic groups, with the Jews on the bottom, and the Italians not far above them. His chipped front tooth and his well-muscled arms, legs and torso, were all a product of him and his Italian-American cousins and friends having to fight their way out of jams. At least that's the story he told me.

And of course, my father changed his name from Felice to Philip. Felice was also his father's, grandfather's, and great grandfather's name. He didn't want me to be named Felice, but he wasn't in the maternity ward when my mother chose my name and filled out the birth certificate. That's why their second born son's name is Junior. Not very Italian-American of them, was it? But why didn't my father change his full name? Why not Philip Pick or Phillip Pickard? Why stop at one name? I always wondered.

As for my mother, born in 1913, she was not a typical girl from an Italian-American background during that time. She grew up in rural Thornton. When I was a kid, we spent most summers with her father in Thornton. My grandfather was a professional by the time my mother was born. A printer and editor, he had formed his own newspaper, which was later bought by, and then folded into, *The Providence Journal.* My mother's older brothers were a lawyer, an insurance executive, and a politico with a seat in the state legislature. As a teenager, my mother had a car and money to buy expensive clothing. She was part of Rhode Island's young yachters, and she played Pro-Am tennis at Newport, along with her affluent cousins from Barrington. She socialized with national sports and entertainment figures. In her twenties, she worked in downtown Providence as a floorwalker for The Peerless Department Store, where she later became a fashion mannequin, and an officer.

Overeducated and pampered, for years my mother dated her soul-mate, whom she nicknamed Sourpuss. He was a playboy from an entrepreneurial family that made money even faster than it produced children riddled with mental illness. After she divorced my father of thirty-five years of marriage, my mother married Sourpuss, whom I'd heard about during my childhood from my mother's tales of her youthful adventures.

My mother told me she had rejected Catholicism at the age of sixteen when a priest in the confessional asked her what she "did with her hands at night." Her response was loud, angry, and unprintable; she attempted to have him arrested. The matter was only hushed up when he was relocated to a distant parish.

After my father's funeral, his long-time attorney told me that when he was young, my mother was the bravest person he'd ever met. "She publicly berated policemen, politicians, military men, and anyone she thought was doing wrong!," he said in wonderment. My mother was not the typical, suffering Madonna in black clothing, who remains silent in the background. I know where my hate for injustice and my big mouth come from.

After my parents wed, they set up house in middle-class, central Queens, nowhere near a Roman Catholic Church, a Catholic school, or an Italian-American neighborhood. Over the years, under my mother's prodding, we moved farther and farther east, until the Nassau County line actually separated our property from our neighbor's. My father once asked my mother why she had no Italian-American friends. And her response was: "You'd like that, wouldn't you? So I would be as brainwashed as they all are by their mothers and the church."

Church attendance in our family was initiated by my father. I went to church with him, while my mother stayed at home to cook Sunday dinner. I remember a minor brouhaha at home, when my older brother joined his best friend's Boy Scout troop, which met at the local Lutheran church. I remember my mother saying, "What's the difference which church he goes to, Phil? They're all pretty much the same and they're all just after your money."

But the final proof that confirmed my mother's Un-Italian-American-ness came from my paternal grandmother, Concetta, who lived on a chicken farm in Thornton until the end of her days at age eighty-nine. She barely spoke English, despite living in the United States for eight decades. She always referred to my mother as "*L'Americana,*" the American woman, a word with many connotations, and not a single one of them good.

❧

However, being Italian-American was sexy, even a little risqué. Popular novels and movies, like *Peyton Place*, always had at least one sexy Italian-American guy who parked cars or bartended at the casino, and who popped all the WASP girls' cherries. It was almost considered an Italian-American public service. The slick guy with smoldering eyes and long, wavy black hair was the stuff of romance magazine legends; he combed his hair so often that it was masturbatory.

Three of my Recco male cousins, Andrew, Matthew and Louis, who were eight to twelve years older than me, were very attractive. As a pre-teen, I remember sitting around their bedroom, watching them get dressed to go out on a Saturday night. It was a lesson in grooming, and a great way for a gay man in training to see how high the bar could be raised.

As a teenager, I had no trouble finding girlfriends because of my Italian-American looks. I always had one, and I was initiated into heterosexuality early and often. Had I gone away to college in Colorado or New Mexico, I might have stood out. However, in New York's Tri-State area, my ethnicity was the norm.

And when, as an adult, I entered gay life in the early 1960's, I encountered no problems in finding boyfriends. I had a well-proportioned, natural, slender body, which was before big muscled men became popular. I had smooth skin, with little body hair, and a full head of dark, curly hair. I also had large, deceptively warm, Italian brown eyes. And during the summertime, I tanned beautifully because of my olive complexion. Whatever I actually thought of my facial features, I knew that some people would brush me off instantly as not conventionally handsome because I did not have the "all-American look."

Soon enough, I would quickly discover an entire subset of gay men, mostly WASPs, but also some Jewish, who were strongly attracted to the Italian-American media-stereotype of the 1950's and 60's. And I must confess that I used my "ethnic card" to my advantage, in order to get laid because I knew that they fantasized about having sex with a "Bensonhurst Guido." These WASPs and Jewish men were handsome architects, doctors, lawyers, actors, etc., who would not have had sex with me otherwise because of their negative stereotypes of Italian-Americans

When I was dating Ed Armour in the early 1970's, he took me to Fire Island, and we were guests of a friend. We were alone most of the week, but on the weekend other guests arrived. Ed introduced me to a gay WASP who immediately assumed that I just got "off the boat" from Italy. He began speaking to me slowly and precisely, so I decided to play along by replying with a thick Italian accent. At the end of that summer season, Ed and I encountered the gay WASP again at the New York City Ballet. While Mr. Bias was carefully introducing me to his companion, Ed interjected, "Marv, did Felice tell you? His novel is a finalist for the Hemingway Award!" Marv looked like he wanted to sink into the ground.

૨૦

After my book, *Art & Sex in Greenwich Village* was published in 2007, I found myself lecturing at various colleges as a "cultural historian." At one of these events, Joe D'Allessandro was also present. After I got over my initial shock that a druggy like him was still alive, he acknowledged me and together we spoke in some detail about the various denizens of Warhol's Factory, where we'd first met. Joe remembered a lot more than I thought he would.

In the late '60s and early '70s, he was "Little Joe," physically perfect and the coolest Italian-American hustler and movie star on the scene, and maybe in the world. When I mentioned my encounter with Joe to old friends, each of them asked the same question, "After all that heroin, how does he look?"

"Surprisingly good," I told them. "Kind of like a trim Italian-American granddad."

"It's those Mediterranean genes," each of them replied the same way. "You Italian-American guys are so lucky."

"Finally!," I thought.

ITALIAN-AMERICAN RECONCILIATION

Frank Anthony Polito

Frank Anthony Polito. Could a name possibly get any more Italian than that? And yet, I sometimes don't feel the least bit *Italiano*. My father is only half Italian, which, doing the math, makes me a quarter. The other nationalities I lay claim to in my genetic pool are Irish and German on my father's mother's side, and English, German, and Canadian on my mother's, the Lillys. Taking this into consideration, I suppose I'm more German than anything else, really, which might explain my fascination with Hitler and the Nazis, Anne Frank and her diary, and *Cabaret* and Christopher Isherwood.

To look at me now, one might see some semblance of Italian heritage in my physical characteristics. My hair is dark (well, now it's graying along the sides, but in general I'd consider it "brown"), and I have a somewhat prominent nose. But growing up, I had white-blond hair and my eyes have always been blue, two traits I inherited from my English-German-Canadian mother, who is really just "American" in my humble opinion. As a kid, my teachers would marvel, "Polito? You're Italian! Your mother must be a wonderful cook." I'm not saying she's untalented in the kitchen, but Mom's idea of "Italian cooking" consists of opening up a jar of Ragu.

Like most of the other quote-unquote Italian Americans who are featured in this collection, whom I presume are Roman Catholic, I was not raised Catholic, so my only memories of altar boys and priests are the ones I created in my perverted little mind. My grandfather *used* to be Catholic. But then in the early 1960s, he and my grandmother divorced, and he got kicked out of the church. *Excommunicated*, I believe they call it. Actually, I don't even know if this is factual. But it sounds good, so it's what I tell people when they ask why I'm not a card carrying Catholic. And yet, somehow I have *tons* of "Catholic Guilt" leftover from my non-Catholic upbringing.

When I came to New York City in the mid-1990s to pursue an acting career, I would often get called in to audition for "Italian" roles. Remember Jackie Aprile Jr. on *The Sopranos*? That could have been me! Instead, the role went to hottie Jason Cerbone, better known as "Luka" from the Suzanne Vega video. Whatever happened to him? Of course, this stemmed from the name printed on the bottom of my headshot: FRANK ANTHONY POLITO. Again, can it get any more Italian? And yet, I would arrive at the casting office wishing I'd purchased a pair of brown contact lenses and dyed my hair darker because every other guy in the room looked like hottie Jason Cerbone.

My Grandpa Polito (Anthony, aka "Tony") isn't even actually Italian. He was born here in America in 1917, as was his older brother Alfonso (aka "Al") in 1915. Grandpa's oldest brother William (aka "Willie") was born in Sicily, as were his parents, my great-grandparents, Frank and Jennie. Still, everyone on the Polito side of the family has that Italian look, with their dark hair, dark eyes, and olive skin. As a child, whenever we'd go to visit my father's family in rural Pennsylvania, I was always the odd one in terms of the way I looked. My dad's cousin, Bonnie, would cook her authentic Italian dinners of spaghetti with "gravy" and chunks of sausage, and crusty Italian bread with *real* butter. Along with our scrambled eggs at breakfast came potatoes fried in olive oil with chunks of *real* garlic that everyone at the table would fight over. On the other hand, at home, Mom would brown hamburger and add it to her jar of Ragu, garlic came in powder form, and our bread was baked by Wonder and slathered with Parkay margarine.

Still, I professed to be Italian, whenever anyone would ask. Like in elementary school, when we studied our "roots," as they called it in the post-Alex Haley generation, I always focused on the Polito side of *mia famiglia*. But I couldn't even trace back any further than Great-grandpa Frank and Great-grandma Jennie, who escaped from Sicily after Great-grandpa Frank betrayed the mafia, so they put a hit out on him, so he and his wife had to flee the country with their newborn son, "Willie." Actually, I don't even think that this is factual, either. But it sounds good, so it's what I tell people when they ask why my great-grandfather emigrated from Italy. (Side note: when Frank and Jennie stopped at Ellis Island in 1914 or thereabouts, their surname was *Ippolito*. But like a lot of other immigrants, somehow it got shortened. When I learned this tidbit as a child, I felt short-changed as there weren't any kids in my class whose last name began with I. How cool would it have been to be unique?)

Little did I know —okay, I *did* know, but the expression is "little did I know" —that at the age of nine I was indeed a unique member of the Polito family because I was the only known homosexual. Well, I wasn't known back then, but.... This brings me to the point of why I'm writing this essay.

I came out as a gay man to my immediate family almost fifteen years ago, and more recently to my mother's side, the Lillys, which came as no big surprise to anybody, and was not a big deal whatsoever. When I was six, my cousins, Donna and Charlene, and I would play *Charlie's Angels* together. Of course, I was always the non-gender specific Kris (aka Cheryl Ladd), just in case my dad would overhear us running around, pointing our finger-guns and calling each other by our character names: *"Cover me, Kris!"*

There have been gay people in the Lilly family for generations. My mother's Uncle Gene was an active participant in the Detroit gay social scene of the 1960s, dressing in drag as his alter ego "Jeannie Harlow," and venturing out to the Ten-Eleven Bar to participate in the drag queen Halloween parade. Mom's older cousin, Roberta (aka "Bobbie") is a lesbian whose former lover was none other than adult film super-star, Nina Hartley, with whom "Bobbie" would appear on national talk shows like *Donahue*, in the 1980s to discuss their non-traditional relationship.

And yet, for the most part, I'm still not open about my sexuality to the Polito branch of my family tree. This stems, I suspect, from the fact that I don't want to disappoint my Italian grandfather and his older brother, Uncle Al, who are both still alive and kicking at the ripe old ages of ninety-five and ninety-seven, respectively. (How about them Polito genes? I only hope their longevity for life gets passed down my way!)

With the publishing of my first novel in June of 2008, I suddenly found myself in the public eye, which is where I've always wanted to be, and the reason I first became an actor. But I've not discussed my creative endeavors with the majority of the folks on my father's side of the family out of fear, worry, and dread that word will get back to my grandfather. As much as I want him to be proud of me, I'm not sure that "Tony" Polito, The Italian Stallion who'd had three different wives and a long-distance girlfriend at the age of eighty, would understand why his oldest grandson wrote a book called *Band Fags!* and wasn't married himself at the age of thirty-eight.

Sadly, this past fall, my grandfather had a stroke. As a result, he's been living with my father's brother and his wife. My Uncle Mike and Aunt Marie are what I like to call ex-hippie-bikers-turned-born-again-Christians. Uncle Mike still has the tattoos on his forearms and he still rides a Harley, but gone is the ponytail he used to sport down his back, and no more does he drink and smoke. He and Aunt Marie go to church every Sunday and Uncle Mike also "ministers" to other ex-hippie-bikers-turned-born-again-Christians. They do *not* know that I'm known to some as "gay author Frank Anthony Polito." Well, not officially.

With the invention of Facebook a few years back, I used my status as "engaged" to my partner of over twenty years to clue in Uncle Mike and Aunt Marie's daughter, my cousin Jennie, when she "friended" me. Curiously enough, I did not accept Aunt Marie's request to connect via social media, though I am friends with my dad's youngest brother Robin's wife, my Aunt Karen, and all of her five *straight* sons. Unless they don't pay that close attention to my updates and postings about my novel, *Band Fags!*, getting banned, and receiving the Lambda Literary Award for its follow up, *Drama Queers!*, they all must know by now which side my crusty Italian bread is buttered on.

Now that my grandfather has taken this turn in terms of his health, I know that his time with us grows short. I hate to think of him leaving this world without knowing who I truly am. And yet, I can't bring myself to broach the subject. Is it because I'm ashamed of being gay? I don't think so.

I think it's because I'm proud of being Italian American.

WHEN ONE (DEAD) GAY ITALIAN AMERICAN SON HELPS ANOTHER

Michael Schiavi

When Michael Carosone and Joseph LoGiudice invited me to contribute to this volume, I was honored but skeptical. First off, I'm only *half* Italian-American, though Michael sweetly insisted that this did not disqualify me. Secondly, I've never given much thought to my ethnic identity. I've built a scholarly reputation on my sexual identity—"gay" is all over the titles of my publications—but the Italian-American part? That was something I noticed mainly on Christmas Eve over long family dinners and memories of my grandmother's baccalà. What could I write about?

Then I had an idea. For months, the prospect of committing this idea to paper gave me atrocious writer's block. It would mean exhuming some long-buried bodies. But I'm glad I've done it. I'm much gladder to have gotten through it. And I have a departed *paisan* to thank for giving it all the happy ending without which you wouldn't be reading a word of what follows.

❧

It's May 1993. I'm twenty-three years old and standing in my mother's kitchen, having flown from New York to Pittsburgh to attend my grandmother's eightieth birthday party. I'm on the phone with my father, who has recently found out that I'm gay and is angrier than I've ever heard him. In his voice all I can hear is ex-Marine, Italian-Catholic bigotry. I'm too unnerved to hear his grief and confusion. He tells me that my news is the hardest thing he's ever endured—harder than his own father's death when he was a year younger than I am. I try to change the subject and tell him about the full-time teaching job I've just landed, my first. He replies tonelessly that this accomplishment doesn't matter, then adds, "I'm sorry if that offends you. I guess I don't give a fuck who I offend anymore." This is the first time I've heard my father use the word "fuck." We're in a new and frightening place.

The next days are awful. Dad drives to my mother's apartment to have it out with both of us. We're to blame, she and I, for this lifestyle choice I've made. (I should explain that while my father is 100% Italian-American, my mother is 100% WASP. Their cultural commonalities could fit on a postage stamp.) A music teacher and choral director, my mother took me to too much theater when I was growing up. Plus, Dad thunders, I'm obviously "doing this" just to upset him. I begin unraveling the fallacies of his argument. How did summer-stock Rodgers and Hammerstein determine my predilection for men? How did my being gay devolve from biology to a pissy pose that I've adopted like the rebellious teen I never was? How could I simultaneously have been *ruined* by my showtune-loving mother and consciously *chosen* to be gay? With these questions boiling in my brain, I keep my mouth shut and try to listen as Dad asks whether I ever had any sexual feelings for girls. Around sixth grade, didn't I notice their development, didn't I feel any spark? I reply truthfully that I did not. I don't tell him how long it took me to recognize my attraction toward other boys. Years of yearning went unnamed, even to myself, because on some hidden level I had been dreading exactly this scene.

The conversation goes nowhere. My father and I are both hurt and outraged. There's nothing more to say.

A couple of days later, we're at Gram's party, where Dad has requested that I not wear an AIDS ribbon. "Some of the family wouldn't understand." He seems terrified that I'm planning to hijack the occasion for a mass coming-out. This couldn't be further from my intention. The immediate family already knows, and for the time being, that's more than enough.

The evening yields an emblematic photo. Someone wanders by our table and snaps a shot of me with my parents. My mother, trying to bridge the sizable gap between Dad and me, has planted one hand on my shoulder and stretched the other out to his. Her maniacal smile is fooling no one. She might as well be screaming, "Wrong?! Wrong?! Nothing wrong here!" Dad looks like he's passing a kidney stone. My grin is sculpted from wire.

Dad and I don't speak for over six months. When we do, I'm still so furious that civility is no more possible than a frank discussion, which, in any event, is not our family style. And we have too much history on this particular subject.

✌

For a while, Dad and I had a kind of gender détente going. Until I was about seven, there was no forcing of boy activities. He would happily get down on the living-room floor with me to draw washers and dryers, two of my early-childhood obsessions. Somewhere there's a photo of him holding me over my fourth birthday cake. I'm in a violet velour suit—gimme a break, it was 1974—clutching my prized possession, a toy coffee pot. A couple of years later, Dad helped me to cut out and color a paper star so that I could make a magic wand. I think I was trying to be the Blue Fairy in *Pinocchio*. Such can only have been the impression of neighborhood boys who saw me traipsing about our backyard, all but levitating on pixie dust as I leveled my wand at planters, turning them into princes.

Then the tug-of-war began, probably around the time the word "faggot" became a daily agony for me at school. Dad was nice about it at first. He loved buying me a baseball, glove, and bat, and we spent hours playing backyard catch. One Sunday, he organized an informal game with me and a bunch of older boys from the block. All of us played with such enthusiasm that by day's end, the baseball had morphed into a battered, broken egg and ended up in the trash, which was fine by me.

I had fun that day, but I much preferred spending my spare time curled up behind the couch with a book. This didn't sit well with my father. Boys were meant to be ballplayers, not bookworms. I swallowed a surprising amount of seven-year-old resentment when he loomed before me, a book in my lap, and informed me that my long-deceased grandfather would have been happy with a son who spent all his time reading. The implication was that Dad was not happy with such a son. I couldn't fathom why reading was such a problem. But I said nothing. There was no way to tell him that, by this time, I spent so much time indoors, in part, because boys my age scared me. They were loud and boisterous and cruel. They called me names and shoved me around. And they seemed so interminably stupid.

My choice of playmates was also a big problem for Dad. A perfect stereotype, I surrounded myself with girls. My father was always friendly to them, but when they left, he sometimes lashed out, especially as I headed toward adolescence with few signs of manliness. The comments got progressively more toxic: Why did I spend so much time with Ashley, my best friend? Was I planning to cut my nails, or paint them? When was I going to "pick up a bat and ball" and "be a man"?

It's hard to fault my father for views that he acquired all too honestly. He grew up in a blue-collar, staunchly Italian-Catholic Pittsburgh suburb of the 1940s and '50s. His father, my aforementioned grandfather, was an Italian immigrant renowned for his ferocious temper and strength. At 5'6", Angelo Schiavi looks pretty unimposing in sepia photos, but according to family lore, he once slammed his fist through a living-room wall. Angelo thought being a man meant smoking a lot, drinking a lot, slaving in construction, and carving a place for himself and his children in America. He was so eager to fit in to American culture that he faux-Anglicized the pronunciation of his surname from the euphonious "Skee-AH-vee" to the indeterminate "Shy-Ă-vee," which my parents use to this day. Years later, my father told me that his father would never have understood the concept of a gay grandson. I wasn't sorry that Angelo had died thirteen years before my birth.

Similarly, Dad's hometown was far from enlightened on boys who didn't toe the masculine line. One Sunday evening when I was twelve, Dad and I found ourselves in the unlikely position of watching *Solid Gold* on TV. (I say "unlikely" because my father's interest in pop music evaporated with the Ink Spots around 1954.) As the Solid Gold Dancers writhed to Laura Branigan's "Gloria," his facial expression soured from stony to revolted. We watched the lithe, spandex-clad male dancers silently until he spat a homophobic put-down. I blurted back that I didn't think there was anything wrong with being gay. I didn't actually have any opinion on the topic, but Dad's remark stung. At that moment, he looked and sounded exactly like the boys who were terrorizing me at school.

My comment triggered a meltdown in the car that night. There certainly *was* something wrong with being gay. Everyone knew that. Gripping the steering wheel, Dad told me the story of Frank, a profoundly effeminate high-school classmate. Frank tried to be friendly to my father, who, thirty years later, recreated Frank's singsong nasal greeting ("Hiii, Jooooeee!") as a deadly faggot lampoon. The school football team took Dad's disgust one step further. They beat Frank so severely that he had to be rescued by the police, who delivered him to his parents' doorstep with a snarling admonition to keep him off the streets for a few days.

This tale was told to me in tones of icy righteousness. It hit much too close to home. Churning stomach acid by the gallon, I screwed up all my courage to ask my father a question. "Do you think that was right?" He glanced away from the road and down at me. "Do I think what was right?" I swallowed hard, feeling such kinship with poor battered Frank that I could barely speak. "Do you think it was right for the football team to beat him up like that?" I didn't hear a word of my father's blustery reply. I was flying on the adrenaline of having protested the abuse of "different" boys. It was my first surge of self-respect.

But it didn't last. Eighth and ninth grades were a nightmare of bullying at school, a fact that I did my damndest to hide from my parents. Living it was bad enough; I certainly didn't want to talk about it. Also, I sensed there wasn't much to be done. This was decades before the "It Gets Better" campaign and the anti-bullying policies that many schools have since adopted to protect their most vulnerable children. In my school, teachers and administrators turned a blind eye and allowed terrorism to flourish. On one of the rare occasions when the subject surfaced at home, my father informed me that the attacks I was suffering were my own fault.

What happened was this: some anonymous thugs had spent weeks vandalizing my locker. I told nobody. Then they stole my winter coat, which brought the whole mess to light. It was the coldest November in years, I couldn't go to school in shirtsleeves, and I needed adult intervention. Mortified, I told my mother what had happened, and she immediately bought me a new coat—but, disregarding my pleas, she also informed my father of what had happened. I then received a livid ninety-minute lecture on the necessity of manly behavior.

There was a modicum of relief in finally discussing the torture that my daily school life had become. But to this day, nearly thirty years later, I don't think I've ever felt the rage that I felt that afternoon. I knew I wasn't to blame for what was happening to me. I knew there was something wrong with adults who allowed children to target other children who had done them no harm. And even now, I can't fully articulate the blind fury that I felt when my father, speculating on the causes of the bullying, commented, "Now, we know there's nothing *wrong* with you." His tone suggested that we knew nothing of the sort. Suddenly we were back in *Solid Gold* territory. At thirteen, I hadn't yet realized my sexuality, so I can't say that I felt my father was criticizing me for something I consciously knew myself to be. I think I was enraged for a range of reasons, none of which I ever really thought through until now. Dad had just demonstrated, yet again, his opinion of non-masculine boys. He was implying that gayness itself was so terrible that it couldn't be named. He was forcing me to muse on what inside *me* was causing other boys to behave so outrageously. He was giving me no sympathy at all. And I was dangerously close to losing control. Near the end of the lecture, Dad sneered at my trembling lip. "Are you gonna *cry* now?" No way would I give him the satisfaction. I replied as evenly as possible. "No."

And that was that. The subject remained taboo for a very long time. When I came out to my father ten years later, we hadn't mentioned homosexuality once in the interim. And after my coming out, we didn't mention it again for another fourteen years.

❧

The silence was just as much my doing as his. After coming out, I retreated completely. For years, I'd been dodging the revelation; once it was made, I couldn't imagine what, if any, step came next. I

seethed when my father insisted on referring to Chris, my first partner, as my "roommate"—whose name he never used during the
three years we were together—but I didn't correct him. Five years
later, when I received my Ph.D. from New York University, I told
my mother to tell my father that my then-partner would be joining
us at graduation and for lunch at Tavern on the Green. I frostily informed her, as if she were to blame, that there would be no euphe-
mistic references to Rick as my "friend." She agreed.

Dad seemed tense at the ceremony, but he was perfectly polite.
I, on the other hand, was a nervous wreck introducing him to Rick.
Here I was, twenty-eight years old, about to collect my doctorate on
the stage of Carnegie Hall, and I still couldn't find a way to discuss
the central facet of my identity with my father. This led to some lu-
dicrous obfuscation on my part when he asked, more than once, the
subject of my dissertation. Its title was *Staging Effeminacy in America,* but I wasn't about to share that factoid with him. Instead, I over-
simplified by telling him the project was about modern American
drama. He knew that doctoral writing was considerably more spe-
cialized than that and asked for clarification. I shrugged it off as "too
technical" to discuss and changed the subject.

I continued this pattern for a very long time. During my six ten-
ure-track years at New York Institute of Technology, where I've
taught since 1998, I published some thirteen articles on gay theatre,
gay film, and gay pedagogy. I gave over twenty conference presenta-
tions and chaired panels on similar topics. As anyone who's ever
gone through the tenure process knows, this is backbreaking work.
It absorbs at least 90% of your energy and 110% of your anxiety. My
father knew that I was slaving away, but he had no idea about what.
When he inquired about the focus of my research, I stammered the
same evasive stupidities that I had used since grad school. When he
urged me to send him my publications, I said I would, but never

followed through. After a while, he stopped asking, and I got huffy. Didn't he care about what I was doing? Looking back, I'm amazed not to have realized that he stopped asking because he never got a real answer. If he knew almost nothing about my life, it was my own sweet fault.

In 2006, Dad underwent successful cancer surgery and moved back in with my mother. During my visits to Pittsburgh, I had always stayed with her and seen my father when he came to the house, or when we went out to family dinners. Now they were back together, so visiting Mom meant visiting Dad. At that time, I was in the middle of a ten-year relationship with Scott, my third partner and the first man to accompany me on biannual family trips. This caused me no end of apprehension: my father in the same house where my same-sex partner and I would be sleeping in the same bed?! But I was mystified by Dad's smooth rapport with Scott. They sat at the dining-room table and talked for hours about politics, history, and academe. I couldn't imagine where my father had found this chatty ease with his son's male partner. At the time, I thought it worked because Scott isn't stereotypically gay. If he'd been at all flaming, I reasoned, my father wouldn't have spent five minutes with him. Now I doubt that interpretation. Dad was justifiably impressed by Scott, whose knowledge of American history, like my father's, is prodigious. He was also charmed by Scott's warm, deferential manner. I think Dad enjoyed talking to Scott simply because he was a generous and informed conversationalist. "Gay" seemed not to enter the picture at all. I very much doubt that it ever came up during their many talks.

It certainly never came up with Dad and me. And I never brought it up. If, after all the past strife about my sexuality, my father was able to be so gracious to my partner, then there was nothing to discuss. We were fine. Problem solved, crisis over.

Crisis over: Yes. Resolution: No. The resolution didn't come until another Italian-American entered my life: Vito Anthony Russo (1946-1990).

૨ა

Vito was the author of *The Celluloid Closet* (1981; revised 1987), the first book to study how Hollywood's systematic denigration of gay men and lesbians directly informed our second-class citizenship for over seventy years. Through hundreds of examples of the laughable sissy, the murderous dyke, the queer psychopath, and the gay suicide, Vito vividly demonstrated how our every appearance in film, the dominant art form of our time, was treated as a joke, a threat, or a subject for pity. From silent films into the 1980s, we were almost never portrayed as complete, healthy human beings capable of living our lives with integrity and hope. When straight audiences saw such images, they had their homophobia justified. When gay audiences saw them, we had our self-hatred reinforced.

Vito was the perfect writer to declare war on this bigotry. He was the son of a fiery mother and a construction-worker father, first-generation descendants of Sicily and Naples who brooked positively no assaults on the family. In East Harlem of the 1950s, when their bookish little boy was attacked on the streets, Annie and Charles leapt to action. Annie proudly recalled pounding a drunken woman who'd dared to slap her son on East 120th Street. And Charles, witnessing an older punk lift his rail-thin son by the neck, raced into the street and nearly put said punk in traction. From his parents, Vito learned two key lessons: take no shit, and take care of your own. He began applying both lessons in early adulthood.

In his early twenties, Vito started to notice the relentless slander that non-heterosexuals had suffered in film. He was determined to change that. *The Celluloid Closet* was born in 1973 as a twenty-minute lecture on gay and lesbian images then available in movies. Analyzing clips from such chestnuts as *Victim* (1961), *The Children's Hour* (1962), *The Killing of Sister George* (1968), and *The Boys in the Band* (1970), Vito informed New York-area college students that his tribe had been mightily maligned by Hollywood. He soon developed a reputation as a passionate speaker with a unique message. Within a few years, he was receiving impressive invitations: the Roxie Theatre in San Francisco, the Fox-Venice in Los Angeles, and the American Film Institute in Washington. He then took the lecture abroad, decrying homophobia in England, Ireland, Switzerland, and Australia. By the end of his life, several years after the book's publication, Vito had perfected a three-hour performance that was without question the most famous gay lecture in the world. Along the way, he had co-founded the Gay and Lesbian Alliance Against Defamation (GLAAD) and the AIDS Coalition to Unleash Power (ACT UP). He was the gay community's most beloved spokesman. Five years after his death from AIDS complications, Academy Award-winning directors Rob Epstein and Jeffrey Friedman adapted *The Celluloid Closet* into a documentary film featuring Vito's good friend Lily Tomlin as the narrator. Vito had passed from man to legend.

I was mesmerized by him. I discovered *The Celluloid Closet* as a closeted college freshman and rabid young film queen. In a lifetime of avid reading, no book had ever touched me so deeply. Staring at the cover, which featured pink- and blue-tinted lesbian and gay couples from *Pandora's Box* (1928) and *Consenting Adult* (1985), I knew instantly that this *paisan* got me. I spent hours randomly flipping through the text. Hundreds of titles and images leapt off the page. Most of the discussion was appalling. I had no idea that what I'd been enduring in school for years had been unfolding for decades on the silver screen. No *wonder* we took so much abuse.

The connection was profound; it was, for me, the realization of a lifetime, as was my immediate identification with this gay Italian-American wiseass. *The Celluloid Closet* was leavened with an abundance of irreverent, audibly homosexual New York humor. At seventeen, I had never met an openly gay person, and I had never been to New York City, but I knew a Manhattan queen when I read one. Vito was speaking my language. Or, rather, he was teaching me a language in which I couldn't wait to become fluent.

It's one of my deepest regrets that I never had the chance to meet Vito. He died when I was twenty, less than a year before I moved to New York to begin graduate studies. But he was never far from my thoughts. Chris, my first partner, knew of my obsession and gave me one of my most cherished gifts, my first copy of *The Celluloid Closet*. Fifteen years later, Scott trumped this kindness with not one, but two autographed copies that he found on E-bay. I, meanwhile, was busily assembling conference talks and a scholarly article, for *Cinema Journal*, on why Vito Russo and his work were still relevant to film studies. Fifteen years after his death, Vito continued to teach me the meaning of productive gay pride.

While researching my article, I interviewed Dr. Larry Mass, cofounder of Gay Men's Health Crisis (GMHC), author of the world's first AIDS article, and husband of Vito's best friend, Arnie Kantrowitz. During our conversation, Larry made a casual comment that changed the direction of my life: "It's nice that you're writing an article on *The Celluloid Closet*, but somebody really should write a full biography of Vito." I munched over that remark for the next six months and then determined, with now-apparent chutzpah, that I would be the ideal candidate.

You know what worried me most about this project? Not having to approach Vito's many famous friends for interviews; not having to juggle greatly increased research demands with an already insane

149

teaching load; not applying for a year's sabbatical and living on a much-reduced salary. No, what worried me most was that this project meant having no choice but to discuss gayness with my father. I couldn't take a year away from teaching and not tell him the reason why. And eventually, if all went well, there would be a biography of a gay-rights giant bearing not just *my* name but *our* name. I was heartened by Dad's good relationship with Scott, but I couldn't imagine his reaction to my latest plans.

I broke the news on a summer visit to Pittsburgh. As usual, my parents and I spent the first evening of my trip catching up at the dining-room table. As usual, Dad asked what I was working on now that the spring semester had ended. I fortified myself with a lethal appletini.

"Well, actually, I'm starting research on a book."

"Oh, really? That's great! What's it about?"

Blood was pounding through my ears at nightclub decibels.

"It's going to be a biography of a man named Vito Russo. He was a famous activist for gay and lesbian rights."

"Oh." There was an uncomfortable pause. "I've never heard of him."

That wasn't surprising. Vito had been dead for almost seventeen years, and though my father is enormously well-read in current events, it's a cinch that Vito never appeared in the Pittsburgh papers. During the 1980s, *The New York Times* was criminally quiet on the subjects of gay rights and AIDS; greater liberalism could hardly be expected in Pittsburgh.

"Well, he wrote a book called *The Celluloid Closet...*" I gave the briefest possible overview of Vito's career, feeling as I often do when teaching gay material to non-gay classes that if I speak as factually and dispassionately as possible, I'll retain maximum interest. This approach grossly underestimated my father's intellect, but there was much more at stake here than an academic project. No less than my coming out had been years earlier, this was a moment of truth. Dad's response was supportive but subdued. My writing a book about Vito Russo meant the beginning of something that was not likely to end anytime soon. He wasn't fully on board.

I had brought DVDs of *The Celluloid Closet* and *Common Threads: Stories from the Quilt* (1989). An Academy Award-winning documentary about the creation of the NAMES Project AIDS Memorial Quilt, *Threads* features Vito as one of six principal narrators who have lost loved ones to the epidemic. I wanted my mother to see *Closet* and *Threads* to get some sense of Vito. My father was a different story. For years, as his hearing waned, he had drastically curtailed his attendance at movies and watching of non-CNN television. So when he declined to watch the two films, there was a potential excuse. I honestly didn't mind. The conversation we'd just had was progress enough.

As I worked on the book's research and writing, I had in mind two principal audiences: the Russo family and my father. They pre-occupied me for a similar reason. Vito's life, like that of most young urban gay men of the 1970s, was mind-bogglingly sexual. For Vito, having sex with as many men as possible, when and wherever he chose, was the best possible way to express Gay Pride. Mainstream society incessantly told him that his attraction to men was an abomi-nation. He was determined to buck that claim at every opportunity. In addition to which, he simply adored sex. He adored men. Jocky blonds were his preference, but he would and did take every other type as well. And he wrote about these adventures in detail. One of the many blessings of being Vito's biographer was that twelve years of his journals are available at New York Public Library (NYPL), thanks to Arnie Kantrowitz. I am not easily shocked, but I spent many an afternoon blushing in the Brooke Russell Astor Reading

Room of NYPL's Manuscripts and Archives Division. (I suspect Mrs. Astor would not have made it to 104 had she flipped through Vito's journals circa 1978-1981.)

Telling Vito's story responsibly meant being honest about his sex life. It was the core of his identity. But it could also have been very upsetting to his family, who were extremely generous to me as I investigated his life. What I learned about his early years in particular could only have come from his brother Charles, his cousin Phyllis (Perky), and his 88-year-old aunt and godmother, Jean. The last thing I wanted was to offend them, so I muted the journals when describing Vito's sex life. Ironically, some of the sweetest compliments I've received on the book have come from gay men of Vito's generation, congratulating me on not whitewashing his sexuality, or the gay '70s, for the sake of propriety. I hope someday they'll take a trip to NYPL to see what "not whitewashed" really looks like.

Then there was my father. As I drafted the book, I continually imagined his reaction. I couldn't help it. Years of censoring myself in his presence had elevated him, in my mind, to my severest critic. What would he think of Vito's sex life? At the same time, I knew that he would read the finished product; he was very proud of my scholarly standing, however little he actually knew of its substance. When The University of Wisconsin Press sent me a contract, my first post-jubilation thought was, "Holy shit. Dad's really going to read this."

Celluloid Activist: The Life and Times of Vito Russo came out in March 2011. I mailed one of the first copies to my mother as a birthday gift. In my inscription to her, I added an awkward P.S.: "Don't hoard this! Share it with Dad, too. ☺" I couldn't have been more disingenuous. Dad was going to read the book, P.S. or no P.S., and I was far from eager to hear his reaction.

I speak to my parents every Sunday by phone. Within a week of their receiving the book, they were passing it back and forth and gushing to me about the first chapter. The arrival of Vito's four grandparents in America, the efforts of two Italian families to forge a life in Manhattan, descriptions of New York City during the 1940s and '50s, decades that my parents remember very well—big hits. Dad was particularly taken with my descriptions of anti-Italian prejudice in East Harlem of the early 20th century. They sounded like what his father had had to endure from Irish squatters in Western Pennsylvania. So far, so good.

Then my parents got to Vito's young adulthood. My mother began this phone conversation sotto voce. "I have to tell you, your father's having problems with your book." Shit.

"Really? What do you mean?" As if I didn't know.

"He put the book down last night and said he doesn't know if he can read any further."

I sighed. "How far did he get?"

He'd gotten up to Vito's friendship with some very raucous, mid-'60s drag queens. These girls were not inclined to watch their mouths and dropped such bons mots as "Don't fuck with my man, you tacky cunt, or I'll put your lights out."

That comment stopped my father cold—my father, the ex-Marine, who, according to my mother, has quite the colorful vocabulary. Not that I've ever heard it; to this day, he remains incredibly decorous around me. Upon reading the terms "fuck" and "cunt" in my book, Dad shut down. He told my mother it was extremely difficult to realize that I had written such language. She reminded him that 1) I was in my forties; 2) I was quoting; 3) I was trying to paint an honest picture of people whose lexicon might not have passed muster in suburban Pittsburgh. He responded that he could only imagine how shocked my aunt, his sister, would be when she read the book.

I got only my mother's version of this conversation. To me, Dad said relatively little—though he did wonder if Vito's propensity to, ahem, "make love" with so many men even long before AIDS indicated some kind of self-destructiveness. I tried to explain the '70s connection of pride with promiscuity, but could tell within a sentence that I had lost him. I let it go.

The following week he dropped a bombshell. "I was talking to your aunt about your book, and I told her she better brace herself for some language that the people we grew up with might not appreciate. And you know what she said to me?" I clenched, waiting to hear how my very Catholic aunt had responded to this warning. "She said, 'Look. My nephew wrote a book, and The University of Wisconsin Press thought it was good enough to publish. Whatever ignorant people might say about it is their problem.'" After picking my jaw off the table, I spluttered, "Well, good for her!" He heartily agreed. My jaw hit the table again. Who was this man?

The next week brought another stunner. Evidently empowered by my aunt, he had continued reading and had a question for me. "How many gay people do you think there are in New York City?" This was the first time I'd ever heard my father use the word "gay." I ignored my trembling and gave him the Kinsey "ten-percent" answer. "Oh, probably about eight hundred thousand."

"You know, I'm really glad to hear that." *What?!* I felt as if I were on another planet, underwater, face-to-face with surprisingly friendly aliens. Dad went on: "I have a feeling that when I was young, a lot of gay people felt really isolated. It's good to know that that's changing."

I went on instant flashback to all of the childhood scenes described above. Had I ever met this man on the other end of the phone? His voice sounded like my father's, but the content was pure Phil Donahue.

Dad ended up reading all of *Celluloid Activist*. Twice. He told me that the first time was just to get the story; the second time was so that he could pick up what he had missed the first time and to appreciate the amount of research I had done. I don't think my mother read the book more than once, not that I expected her to. But my father? *Twice?!*

Since he's read the book, few Sundays go by without some reference to gay rights. Dad almost always initiates these conversations, though I toss in occasionally, too. We've had ripe material over the past year. The homophobic rhetoric of such loons as Michele Bachmann, Rick Santorum, Newt Gingrich, and Mitt Romney has provided Dad and me with endless fodder. In one way, his reactions to them are true to form. My father is a dyed-in-the-wool FDR Democrat. He was born during the heyday of the New Deal and has always believed passionately that government exists to help the less fortunate. Nixon, Reagan, and the Bushes are Satan to him. Now he has extra reason to loathe them and their ilk. They go out of their way to discriminate against his son.

And yet I can't help but wonder what prompted this total about-face. In part, it has to be paternal pride. I'm the first person in our family to publish a book, so no matter the topic, Dad was going to give in eventually. His change must also come from shifting social attitudes. In the past year, as the issues of gays in the military and gay marriage have never faded from the news, my book's timing couldn't have been better (or less intentional, to be sure). Maybe Dad's change evinces an "evolution" of the sort that Barack Obama has been undergoing for the past eighteen months, culminating in his belated endorsement of gay marriage.

I also can't help but feel that Vito's ethnicity has something to do with all this. I think it mattered deeply to my father to read about the blood-and-guts journey of a gay Italian-American man who changed the world before being cut down at the age of forty-four—just two years older than I am now. He must also have been touched to read about Vito's relationship with his parents. They, too, had enormous initial difficulty with their gay son. Much screaming and physical violence, which never played a part in my own story, preceded acceptance. In Annie Russo's case, ultimate "acceptance" meant trips to Fire Island and countless cabaret shows in Greenwich Village with her son, along with livid letters to editors in protest of homophobia and AIDS-phobia. All that from a little old Italian lady just twelve years my father's senior.

Dad must have been impressed by all of this—or so I surmise. Remember, we don't talk about feelings. I doubt we ever will. But I couldn't be more grateful for this new relationship with my father. And I must thank a gay Italian-American hero for enriching my life far more than he could have imagined.

SUNDAY DINNERS

Frank Spinelli

My father passed away unexpectedly from heart failure in 2009 when I was forty-two years old. At the time, I was a physician in private practice and had just moved in with my partner, Chad, happily settled in a relationship that for the first time seemed mature. We had been dating a year when my father got sick.

After suffering from a prolonged attack of gout, my father scheduled a consultation with a podiatrist who recommended a bone biopsy. I was visiting my parents' home in Staten Island for our once-a-month Sunday dinner when he informed me he was having surgery that very week.

"Why didn't you tell me what was going on before you decided to have an operation?" I asked.

"Your father made the appointment himself," replied my mother anxiously. "I told him to talk to you first. Didn't I say that Angelo?"

"Why do I need to check with him first?" he shouted. "You don't understand. None of you people understand the pain I'm in. Why don't you just leave me alone?"

"Come into the city," I suggested. "Let me have one of my colleagues take a look at you."

"No," he said adamantly. Then he looked up at the ceiling with his arms outstretched. "Jesus Christ, I wish the man upstairs would just take me already."

After the operation, the surgeon notified me that the bone in his toe was severely infected, a condition known as osteomyelitis.

"You're father will need a prolonged course of intravenous antibiotics," he explained. "Unfortunately, he'll have to go to a subacute care facility. The good news is that he'll get physical therapy while he's there."

My sister, Maria, flew up from Alabama with her four children once my father was transferred to the rehab center. Every day, my mother, two sisters, brother-in-law, one niece and three nephews visited my father out of loyalty and love because he was the head of our family. We stood around his bed trying our best to lift his spirits, but within days after the surgery, my father grew even more hostile toward the rehabilitation staff. Frequently, he argued with the nurses and refused to take part in the required daily exercises.

"Dad, you have to do what they tell you to do," I insisted.

"The only thing I have to do is pay taxes and die," replied my father.

I shook my head in quiet defeat. That evening, I rode the ferry back to Manhattan concerned that my father's inability to understand his condition was going to hinder his progress. I was reminded of the time he was admitted to St. Vincent's Hospital ten years earlier where he underwent open heart surgery to replace four occluded vessels and a malfunctioning aortic valve. As the cardiothoracic surgeon explained the procedure, my father nodded his head while I stood there wondering if he had any idea at all what was about to happen. But that was just like my father not to ask questions, so that he didn't seem ignorant. Growing up on a farm in Italy, he never went to school and therefore couldn't read or write. Often my sisters and I had to fill out his applications or write out checks for him to sign. Over the years he learned the alphabet by watching *Wheel of Fortune*, but there were certain things even a game show couldn't teach him. Not wanting anyone to think he was dumb, my father often pretended to understand. Unfortunately, it was this particular characteristic of his personality that would eventually lead to his downfall. Riding the ferry that night, I experienced the first inkling that my father might not leave the rehabilitation center alive.

Several days later, Maria returned to Alabama because the children had to go back to school. My father's condition deteriorated rapidly the day after they left. On July 12th, the doctor on call at the rehabilitation facility contacted me. "You're father is experiencing progressive shortness of breath," explained Dr. Shevamundi. "I'm going to transfer him to the emergency room."

"Yes," I said. "That's a good idea."

Standing in my living room with my cell phone still held up to my ear, I looked over at Chad who was listening from the bedroom doorway. "Toe surgery," I said. "This is the kind of stupid shit that's going to kill my dad. Why didn't they just chop it off? He doesn't need that toe. He's seventy-seven."

Five days later, he died. At the wake, I kept a watchful eye on my weeping mother, trying to imagine the depth of her grief at having lost her husband of over fifty years, a man she met at eighteen years old.

My parents were born in the same small town of Teggiano, in the province of Salerno. Michelina Cirone was studying for a final exam at school when her cousin, Pep, his wife, Antoinette, and her brother, Angelo, who was visiting from America, paid her a visit. Angelo, who was twenty-three years old and single, was under strict orders from his father to find a wife on his trip back to his hometown. However, my mother had no interest in meeting him, even when Pep described Angelo as a wealthy and handsome man from New York City. Of all people, it was her best friend, Pina, who convinced her to have coffee with Angelo once she finished her exam. Reluctantly, Michelina agreed out of respect for her older cousin, but the meeting didn't go well. Afterward, Michelina described Angelo as a pompous "pseudo-Americano," whom she had no interest in seeing again.

The next day when Michelina returned to her parents' home for the holidays, she found her mother, six aunts, and her grandmother waiting for her in the kitchen, dressed in black from head to toe. Immediately, she knew what this was all about: an Italian tribunal had been assembled to rectify this matter. That night, Michelina would have little to say, but much to consider. Of course, there was plenty of cooking in preparation for the holidays, but the women used this opportunity, wisely, to convince Michelina that she should thoroughly consider Angelo's impending marriage proposal.

Sitting at the table with her grandmother, Michelina watched as the old woman rolled dough for the zeppoles. "You make them into a ring like this," she said. "Then you watch them as they fry in the oil, but don't let them burn."

"I want to finish school," said Michelina, poking at the rings as the bubbled up in the boiling pot of oil. "And what do we know about this man?"

"Don't you want to have a family?" asked her grandmother, cutting the thin roll of dough into sections. "Finding a good man is hard enough; finding one that can take care of you," she said, while waving a floured finger, "now that's priceless." Although Michelina would continue to argue, she knew her fate was sealed like an uncooked ring of dough awaiting the fryer.

Seventeen days after their first introduction, Michelina Cirone boarded a train for Pompei, where she married Angelo Spinelli. There was no traditional first date and there would be no graduation. She never even found out how she did on her final exam. Later that summer, Michelina traveled to America by herself to meet her husband in New York City, but was horrified to learn that she had been misled. Angelo was far from rich, and Michelina found herself alone in a new country with a different language to learn and a husband she had to help support. For weeks, she cried, cursing her family, her husband and even God. Yet, despite everything she remained devoted to Catholicism and always respected her husband and her parents.

As children, my parents were taught to show respect in the way they spoke and behaved. Growing up, my sisters and I were expected to abide by these same rules, regardless if we agreed with them or not. Disrespecting my parents was not only considered a sin, it was seen as disloyal and ungrateful. While I lived at home, I obeyed my parents. Once I moved out of their house, I found it difficult to visit them because I was still closeted; returning home for Sunday dinners meant keeping this secret from them because my parents considered homosexuality a sin. Over the years, I grew to resent them for this. Before I told them that I was gay, the thought of making the trip to Staten Island for Sunday dinner caused me so much anxiety that I could barely sleep the night before. So I avoided Sunday dinners as much as possible.

My own experience at my father's funeral was less emotional than my mother's. At that time, I was an HIV and had acquired the self-preserving art of detachment as a way to cope with death. But there was more to it than that. Once I told my parents I was gay, they struggled for years to accept it. They finally relented only after I started dating Chad, but by then, the damage seemed somewhat irreparable. For many years, I felt emotionally detached from my family because I was gay, and their inability to accept my sexuality acted as a wedge that loyalty or love could not repair. When the funeral was finally over, I quickly slipped back into my busy life, and was propelled by a need to put the entire event behind me.

A year later, while seeing patients in my office, I received a troubling call from Chad. "I don't feel well," he said.

"You're probably exhausted," I offered. "Remember, you came home late last night after a four-hour train ride. Did you eat breakfast?"

"No," he said.

"Eat something," I insisted, sounding frighteningly like my mother.

Half an hour later, I received a text from Chad. It read, "I feel like I want to throw up." Without a second thought, I went home. Perhaps I was channeling my mother, or I had lived long enough with him to know that he hardly ever complained. By the time I arrived at the apartment, I found him lying in bed. A brown pool of vomit was on the floor next to him. Our dog, Hoffman, was in the living room, whimpering. "How do you feel?" I asked Chad.

"A little better," he replied.

Like my mother, my first instinct was to clean. I frantically began mopping up the floor with a dishtowel. Then I disposed of it directly into the washing machine. When I returned to the bedroom, I noticed Chad's left eye was closed. "What's wrong?"

"I have a terrible headache," he said, slurring his words.

In that moment, I felt conflicted in a way I had never known. On one hand, I wanted to continue acting as my mother, cleaning up the mess to restore order. And yet, the other part of me--the doctor--clearly saw that my next decision was the most crucial one because it seemed as though Chad's condition was about to spiral out of control.

In the end, the doctor won, and we went to the hospital. Once we arrived in the emergency room the events unfolded quickly. Doctors and nurses descended upon Chad, who by now was unable to walk on his own. I stood back helplessly watching while I tried to think of a simple reason to explain his symptoms. But my mind was blank. I was blank. Several minutes later, a thin, pale doctor rushed toward me and introduced himself as the neurology fellow.

"We think your partner suffered a subarachnoid hemorrhage. He has all the classic signs: acute onset, headache, and unsteady gait." I listened while staring at him with one eye, and with the other eye, I watched Chad being wheeled away. "They're taking him for a CAT Scan," he added.

I nodded and hurried to catch up. I wanted to see Chad. I was concerned about how much he knew and wondered if he was afraid. Up ahead, I saw them wheel him into the CAT scan suite. Once he was secured onto the conveyer, I whispered, "How are you?" He winced. His left eye was still closed shut. I crumbled inside.

Through the observation window, I watched as Chad's body was slowly transported head-first into a large, metal doughnut. The neurology fellow urged me to have a seat. "There's nothing you can do," he said. "We'll know more in a few minutes." I finally conceded and sat down. To distract myself, I began to organize by making a mental list:

1. Collect Chad's clothing;
2. Call Eric and have him pick up the dog; and
3. Call Chad's parents in Arizona. No. Don't call them until you know more.

After a series of tests that included blood work, a lumbar puncture, and two negative CAT scans, Chad's doctors were unable to find a cause for his symptoms. The neurology team recommended a neurosurgical consultation. I agreed. Soon after, a tall, Romanian doctor arrived and examined Chad. Once he reviewed all the studies, he suggested a full angiogram of Chad's head and neck. I knew what that entailed. I also knew that the risks included internal bleeding, stroke, and death. Yet, despite all my education and experience,

I hesitated because they were talking about *my* Chad. "I think we should get a second opinion."

"I don't suggest you wait," said the neurosurgeon. Then he pulled me far enough away so that Chad couldn't hear. "Stop thinking of him as your partner. You know the facts. If this were anyone else, what would you advise?"

Fifteen minutes later, I was sitting alone in a room while a doctor whom I met twenty minutes earlier was injecting dye into the arteries of Chad's brain. It was late. I should have been home making dinner. Instead, I was waiting for a neurosurgeon to tell me what was wrong with my partner. A feeling of panic enveloped me like a heavy blanket, and instinctively, I reached for my cell phone and dialed the only person I knew who would understand.

"That's all I know," I said.

"But how did this happen?" asked my mother.

"I'm not sure."

"I'll call your sister Josephine. We'll come to the city and wait with you."

"No, don't come. Just talk to me so I don't stare at my watch."

"Don't be ridiculous! We can be in the city in twenty minutes. You shouldn't be alone."

It was comforting to know that my mother cared. It was also the first time she ever responded in such a way that made me believe she saw us as a real couple. Listening as she tried to console me, I found it difficult to remain composed. The parallels between this situation and my father's were obvious, even though I did not want to believe it. I suppose that is why I called her in the first place.

I looked up at the neurosurgeon who was turning the corner. "Mom, I have to go."

He loomed over me and proudly announced, "Chad had a stroke."

"What?!"

"Come, I'll show you."

The Romanian moved with long determined strides back to the interventional radiology suite. I rushed after him. Inside the technician's room, he pointed to the monitor. I stared at a large screen displaying the outline of Chad's head. His face was replaced by a reticulum of arteries that looked like leafless white branches. The neurosurgeon identified a small area that had been occluded.

"How did a clot get there?" I asked.

"Chad said he was traveling for work yesterday. Perhaps he developed a clot in his leg."

"And it went all the way up to his brain?"

The neurosurgeon scowled when I questioned him. Reaching for his lab coat, he said, "With physical therapy, he'll be able to walk with a cane."

"Did you tell him that?"

"No," he responded.

"Thank you for all your help," I said, reaching out my hand, "but if you don't mind I'd rather if you let me tell him."

Later that night, Chad was moved up to the Neurological Intensive Care Unit. I stayed with him until he fell asleep. The view from his room overlooked the East River. Across the water, I could see the old neon Pepsi Cola sign. I remembered my father once told me that it was Joan Crawford's idea to erect the sign at that exact location as a way to remind the Manhattan residents which soda to buy. It was times like these when I missed my father the most.

Once I returned home that night, I called my mother. We talked, as I lay in bed, alone in the dark. "They'll start physical therapy tomorrow. It's important they begin as soon as possible. What kills me is that Chad is the healthiest person I know. It doesn't make sense."

"Well, at least he's stable now," she said, encouragingly. "How are you?"

"I'm okay. It's weird being alone in the apartment; no dog, no Chad."

"I know. It's not easy to be alone when you're used to living with someone. Sometimes I still can't fall asleep in our bed. Most nights, I sleep in your sister's old room."

"It must have been difficult for you when dad died. I'm sorry I wasn't around more."

"I understand. You have your own life, but treasure each day because life is short."

Ultimately, Chad was diagnosed with a common congenital heart defect medically referred to as a patent foramen ovale. This hole in his heart was the likely culprit that caused the clot to lodge temporarily in his brain.

Two days later, Chad was discharged from the hospital, and like the neurosurgeon predicted, he walked out using a cane. Once he was home, however, he set it aside and never touched it again. That weekend, when I saw it resting in the corner of our bedroom, my mother's words echoed in my head. Now I understood better. Treasuring each day I had with Chad was half of it. The other part now served as a reminder that I had rediscovered a parent's love. For years, it was easier for me to hate my parents because they rejected me for being gay. However, it was more difficult for me to understand that their beliefs had been engrained in them from the time that they were able to understand right and wrong. My father was gone. It was too late to reconcile with him, but I wasn't going to make that same mistake with my mother.

That Sunday, Chad and I made the journey to Staten Island for dinner. Explaining his diagnosis and miraculous recovery was difficult, but once my mother understood the basics, she simply looked at me and joked, "What, your love wasn't enough to fill the hole in his heart?"

"Apparently not," I said. "He still has to decide whether he's going to have the procedure to close it."

"What's there to decide?" she asked. "You can't walk around with a hole in your heart."

I looked at Chad and offered him a nod of concurrence. He smiled politely and said, "I've been walking around with this hole my entire life. I'm not convinced that's what caused the stroke."

"Are you crazy? You're closing that hole," said my mother, squeezing his chin. "You think my son and I intend to live each day worrying you might have another stroke? Not on your life. That's it. End of discussion. Now let's eat."

Listening to my mother, I found myself smiling. I looked over at Chad and whispered, "That's how Italians say welcome to the family."

HI, MY NAME IS TONY TRIPOLI

Tony Tripoli

Hi, my name is Tony Tripoli. I'm a hilarious out gay comic and writer. I'm the head writer for the television show, *Fashion Police*, with Joan Rivers. I've also appeared on the TV shows *Two and a Half Men, Joan and Melissa: Joan Knows Best, Kathy Griffin: My Life on the D-List,* and a bunch of those clips on the E! Channel and TV Guide Channel.

When I was asked to write about being an Italian American, two thoughts immediately popped in my head: 1) Go hide the bottle of *Riunite* in the door of my fridge, and 2) Google a bunch of Italian American shit.

The truth is, I don't feel Italian American. Perhaps it's because I make such a good living from feeling gay. But, that aside, I truly am Italian American. I mean, I don't beat my wife, but you can just tell by my physical features: dark wavy hair, solid jaw line, and full eyebrows-- and that's eyebrows with an "s," because there are two. And I don't look my age because of my thick, oily skin that is resistant to wrinkles. It's oily skin, not Botox!

Then there's my ass. The Italian ass is a thing of beauty. A gift, really. My family is from Sicily, so you know: bam! My ass is so big that when I'm tan, I have zero chance of getting a cab. We are the only white men with this ass. The Greeks didn't inherit it; if they did, they would've invented butt fucking even sooner. Neither did the Spaniards inherit this ass, and not the Czechs, not even the Croatians, and they're only 250 miles away, which is like the size of nine of my asses. But with great power comes great responsibility. And I have devoted my adult life to only using my ass for good, not evil. Sometimes it's a very fine line. That's when you know you're doing it right.

There is one thing about Italians that I have never understood, though: their love, to an almost religious degree, of *The Godfather* films. Okay, not the last one, but the first two.

I mean, these guys were gangsters, killers, crooks, wearers of polyester pants. Why the obsession? It's like all the rappers and their love for *Scarface*. He was an asshole, and he died!

But at least Scarface fucked Michelle Pfieffer at her hottest. *The Godfather* movies had Talia Shire. Um, no thanks. She's like Shelly Duvall, but somehow, less fuckable.

People often ask me how an Italian American kid from Phoenix can write jokes for a comedy legend like Joan Rivers. But, to me, it makes complete sense. Let's be honest: Italians and Jews are the same; the Italians just have better food.

So, my dream is a simple one, and it's a typical Italian one: Respect. I want to be remembered as one of the great Italian men of all time, like Michelangelo Buonarroti, Leonard da Vinci, Christopher Columbus, or ... Donatella Versace. But, my name is Tony Tripoli.

CONTRIBUTORS

MICHAEL CAROSONE is a writer, a poet, an adjunct professor, a librarian, and an activist for gay rights, human rights, animal rights, and environmental rights. He has published poems in *Gay City Volume 1, Gay City Volume 2, Gay City Volume 3*, and *Avanti Popolo: Italian American Writers Sail Beyond Columbus*; essays in *White Crane, Strangers to These Shores*, and various anthologies; and articles in *Gay City News* and *The Huffington Post*. He was awarded the Editors' Poetry Prize for his published work in *Gay City Volume 2*. He has given readings and discussions, and presented papers at conferences. Michael earned a Bachelor of Arts degree and a Master of Arts degree in English, Master of Science degree in Education, and a Master of Science degree in Library and Information Sciences. He is pursuing his Doctor of Education (Ed.D.) degree in English Education at Teachers College of Columbia University, and his dissertation will focus on incorporating marginalized literatures and writers—Queer and Italian American—into the English classroom, in grades K-12 and at the college level. Michael's primary interest is studying, researching, and writing about marginalized literatures, voices, and peoples. Born and raised in Brooklyn, New York, he now lives in the Hell's Kitchen neighborhood of Manhattan, with his partner, Joseph LoGiudice. For more information on Michael, please visit his Web site: michaelcarosone.com.

JOHN D'EMILIO, PH.D., is a pioneer in the developing field of gay and lesbian studies. He is the author or editor of more than half a dozen books, including *Sexual Politics, Sexual Communities: The Making of a Homosexual Minority in the United States; Intimate Matters: A History of Sexuality in America* (with Estelle Freedman); *Lost Prophet: The Life and Times of Bayard Rustin*; and *The World Turned: Essays on Gay History, Politics, and Culture*. D'Emilio has won fellowships from the Guggenheim Foundation and the National Endowment for the Humanities; was a finalist for the National Book Award; and received the Brudner Prize from Yale University for lifetime contributions to gay and lesbian studies. In 1973, while a graduate student, he helped found the Gay Academic Union, a national organization of faculty, graduate students, and independent researchers. A former co-chair of the board of directors of the National Gay and Lesbian Task Force, he was also the founding director of its Policy Institute. *Intimate Matters* was quoted by Supreme Court Associate Justice Anthony Kennedy in the 2003 *Lawrence v. Texas* case, the historic decision that declared state sodomy statutes unconstitutional. When not working, he watches old movies, solves sudoku puzzles, and searches for New York style pizza in Chicago.

CHARLES DERRY, PH.D., was born of an Italian mother and an Irish father. He is Professor Emeritus at Wright State University. The author of several books of film and cultural criticism, including *Dark Dreams 2.0: A Psychological History of the Modern Horror Film* and *The Suspense Thriller: Films in the Shadow of Alfred Hitchcock*, Derry's fiction and criticism have appeared in *The Gay and Lesbian Review, The Portland Literary Review, The Harrington Gay Men's Fiction Quarterly, The Chiron Review, Writers' Forum*, and in the anthologies: *Contra/Diction* and *Reclaiming the Heartland: Lesbian and Gay Voices from the Midwest.* Derry's cancer memoir "A Year Like Any Other" appeared in *The Sun.* He was nominated for a Pushcart Prize for his fiction in *The Chattahoochee Review*, and is also the screenwriter of several short films, including *Cerebral Accident, Joan Crawford Died for Your Sins*, and *The First Great Lesson of My Life.* He lives in Ohio, but also spends time in the California desert. He is currently working on a multi-generational novel set in Cleveland, Ohio, about the Sicilian immigrant experience.

GEORGE DE STEFANO is a New York-based writer, specializing in culture, politics, and sexuality. He is the author of *An Offer We Can't Refuse: The Mafia in the Mind of America* (Farrar, Straus, Giroux), and a contributing author to the collections *Mafia Movies: A Reader* (University of Toronto, 2011) and *The Essential Sopranos Reader* (University of Kentucky Presses, 2011). His writing on gay issues has appeared in *The Advocate, The Gay and Lesbian Review Worldwide*, and *Gay City News.* He writes features and criticism for online and print publications, including music and arts criticism for *PopMatters* and *Rootsworld*; book reviews for *The New*

York Journal of Books; and features, reviews, and op-eds for *I-Italy* and *The Italian American Review.*

JOSEPH A. FEDERICO is a published author and editor. His first book, *Images of America: Galloway Township,* was published in March of 2011. He co-authored the project with his longtime boyfriend. Joseph runs a freelance editorial services business, and is the editor-in-chief of a men's lifestyle magazine. He holds Italian family traditions close to his heart, and wishes that every gay Italian American man could be as lucky as he is to have such a supportive family.

JOSEPH A. LOGIUDICE, L.M.S.W., is a social worker, writer, and an educator. He is the Senior Consultant of Reasonable Accommodations at the New York City Human Resources Administration/Department of Social Services, where he trains and consults on disability law, and determines reasonable accommodations for clients. He is an adjunct lecturer of social work at New York University's (NYU) Silver School of Social Work and Touro College's Graduate School of Social Work, where he teaches courses on social work policy. Joseph's scholarly interests include the intersection of disability and Lesbian, Gay, Bisexual, Transgender, and Queer (LGBTQ) policies and practices, and he has presented on these interests at various conferences. An essay he has written, "Achievement Motivation of College Students with Disabilities: Implications for Policy and Practice," is being published in a textbook on social work policy and practice. Joseph is a committee member on the Council on Social Work Education's Council on Disability and Persons with Disabilities. He is a doctoral student at The City University of New York's Graduate Center, where he studies and researches issues ranging from the implementation of the Americans with Disabilities Act (ADA), mental health policy, and gay men's issues. Joseph received a Master of Social Work degree from NYU's Silver School of Social Work, and a Bachelor of Arts in Psychology from Columbia University. He aspires to become a life-long advocate for those individuals without a "voice" by writing, presenting, and teaching about their lives. He lives with his partner, Michael Carosone, in New York City, and loves his New York City life—a place saturated with eccentric, witty, and interesting people.

MICHAEL LUONGO is an adjunct professor at New York University, teaching travel writing. He is a freelance journalist, editor, and photographer. His travel writing and/or travel photographs have appeared in *The New York Times, Conde Nast Traveler, National Geographic Traveler, Out Traveler, The Gay and Lesbian Review, Gay City News,* and The National Italian-American Foundation's *Ambassador* magazine, to name a few. He is the author, editor, or co-editor of several travel books, including *Gay Tourism: Culture, Identity and Sex* and *Gay Travels in the Muslim World.* He also wrote a novel, *The Voyeur,* which was published by Alyson Books in 2007. Previously, he developed and was editor of the Out in the World imprint for gay and lesbian travel literature for Haworth Press. Luongo has traveled to more than 80 countries and all seven continents, with a geographic concentration in Latin America and the Middle East. He has written extensively on culture, tourism, and human rights in the context of war, focusing on Iraq and Afghanistan. He was the 2011 LGBT Journalist of the Year for the National Lesbian and Gay Journalist Association, winning the Sarah Pettit Memorial Award for Excellence in LGBT Media. He was also the winner of the Grand Prize in Travel Journalism Award. Other awards for his work have been given by the Society of Professional Journalists, the Society of American Travel Writers, and the American Society of Journalists and Authors. His photographs of Rome's World Pride were exhibited at the New York City LGBT Center. He earned a bachelor's degree in Communications, with a minor in English, from Rutgers University, and a master's degree in Urban Planning from Rutgers University's Bloustein School of Planning and Public Policy, with a research concentration on tourism and gay urban spaces. His published master's thesis was on gay sex tourism in New York. Luongo lives in Manhattan. He is Italian-American on his father's side. For more information, visit his Web sites: www.michaelluongo.com and www.gayguido.com.

DAVID MASELLO writes about art and culture for *The New York Times, Town & Country, House Beautiful, Fine Art Connoisseur,* and many other periodicals and Web sites. He has held senior editor positions at several magazines, including *Town & Country, Travel & Leisure,* and *Country Living.* Masello is also a widely published essayist and poet, with works appearing regularly in literary journals and anthologies. He is the author of two books of nonfiction about art and architecture, and has recently completed a new play.

TOMMI AVICOLLI MECCA is a native of Philadelphia. He has been writing ever since he was 10 years old, and produced plays that he and his young friends staged in a neighbor's yard. First published in the poetry pages of his neighborhood weekly (the *South Philly Review/Chronicle*) in the late 60s, he went on to become an editor of the *Philadelphia Gay News*, and a reporter for the *SF Bay Times*. His plays have been produced in Philadelphia, New York, and San Francisco. His 1985 autobiographical work, *Giving Voice*, was received with critical acclaim at Philadelphia's Studio 5. His later updating of that work, *Italian.Queer.Dangerous*, played to sold-out performances and garnered rave reviews in San Francisco's Jon Sims Center in 2004. He is the author of *Between Little Rock and a Hard Place*. He is the co-editor of *Hey Paesan!: Writings by Lesbians and Gay Men of Italian Descent;* and *Avanti Popolo: Sailing beyond Columbus;* and the editor of *Smash the Church, Smash the State: The Early Years of Gay Liberation,* He currently lives in San Francisco and writes a regular column for the online publication *Beyondchron.org.*

JOE OPPEDISANO was born in upstate New York to a typical Italian American family, raised Roman Catholic, and discovered at a very young age that he was gay, which was a realization that clashed with every single thing that he had been taught during his youth. He is a photographer who studied art and fashion at the Fashion Institute of Technology of the State University of New York, when he moved to New York City at the age of 17. He also studied art history for a year in Florence, Italy, where he was given his first break when he was discovered by designer Romeo Gigli. He worked as a fashion editor and stylist for various magazines, including: *Vogue, L'Uomo Vogue, W, WWD,* and *New York Times.* At 30 years old, he picked up a camera and shot his first billboard within the first six months of his career as a photographer. He has published two photography books of erotic male art, and his third book, *j/o,* will be available in October of 2012.

FRANK ANTHONY POLITO is a New York City-based writer. His published novels include: *Band Fags!* (InsightOut Book Club's "Best Fiction" for 2008), *Drama Queers!* (Lambda Literary Award, 2009), *Remembering Christmas* (featuring the sequel to *Band Fags!*), and the young adult novel, *Lost in the '90s*. Frank holds an Master of Fine Arts in Dramatic Writing from Carnegie Mellon University, and a Bachelor of Fine Arts in Theatre from Wayne State University. He grew up in the Detroit suburb of Hazel Park, and currently resides in Sunnyside, Queens, with his partner, Craig Bentley. For more information, visit his Web site: www.frankanthony polito.com.

FELICE PICANO is the author of twenty-five books of poetry, fiction, memoir, nonfiction, and drama. His work is translated into many languages; several titles were national and international bestsellers, and four plays have been produced. He is considered a founder of modern gay literature, along with the other members of the Violet Quill. Picano also began and operated the SeaHorse Press and Gay Presses of New York for fifteen years. His first novel was a finalist for the PEN/Hemingway Award. Since then he's been nominated for and/or won dozens of literary awards, including a Lambda Literary Foundation Pioneer Award in 2009. His most recent work includes: *True Stories: Portraits from My Past, Contemporary Gay Romance*, and *Twelve O'clock Tales*. His fantasy novella, *Wonder City of the West*, will be published in late 2012. Picano's blog appears on the *HuffingtonPost.com*. Recent stories, essays, and reviews can be found at www.felicepicano.net.

MICHAEL SCHIAVI is Professor of English and Coordinator of English as a Second Language at New York Institute of Technology's Manhattan Campus, where he has taught since 1998. He is the author of *Celluloid Activist: The Life and Times of Vito Russo* (University of Wisconsin Press), and his articles have appeared in such publications as *Cinema Journal, Theatre Journal, Modern Drama*, and *College Literature*. He also appears as Vito Russo's biographer in the documentary *Vito* (HBO / Automat Pictures, 2012).

DR. FRANK SPINELLI, M.D., F.A.C.P., is a board certified internist at Chelsea Village Medical in Manhattan. He is an Associate Clinical Professor at New York Medical College, and the author of *Advocate Guide to Gay Men's Health and Wellness*, which was published in 2008 by Alyson Books. He contributes to *The Huffington Post* and appears monthly on Sirius Radio's *Morning Jolt*. In 2012, he was featured in two documentaries, *Positive Youth*, and the Emmy nominated *30 Years from Here*.

TONY TRIPOLI grew up in Phoenix, Arizona, and moved to Los Angeles in 1989, to attend the acclaimed American Academy of Dramatic Arts. Immediately upon graduation, he put his incredibly prestigious and expensive degree to use by moving to Japan to work for Tokyo Disneyland. You can imagine how thrilled his Mom was. He followed that up with a stint as a Chippendale (yeah, that's right... the strippers), and, in a real moment of pride, sang Cole Porter songs for the American Plumber's Association, on stage with a dozen toilets. He has played single-dimensional gay guys on such hit TV shows as *Fashion House* with Bo Derek and Morgan Fairchild, and *Two and a Half Men* with Charlie Sheen and Jon Cryer. He also appeared on *Kathy Griffin: My Life on the D-List*. Tony writes hilarious one-liners for Joan Rivers, which she uses in her act, on her reality show, and on *Fashion Police*. He was also a staff writer on Style Network's hit show, *The Dish*. For more information, visit his Web site: http://tonytripoli.com.

VIA FOLIOS

A refereed book series dedicated to the culture of Italians and Italian Americans.
For a complete list of titles, visit: www.bordigherapress.org.

DANIELA GIOSEFFI, *Escaping La Vita Della Cucina*, Vol. 85. Essays & Creative Writing. $22

MARIA FAMÀ, *Mystics in the Family*, Vol. 84. Poetry, $10

ROSSANA DEL ZIO, *From Bread and Tomatoes to Zuppa di Pesce "Ciambotto"*, Vol. 83. $15

LORENZO DELBOCA, *Polentoni*, Vol. 82. Italian Studies, $15

SAMUEL GHELLI, *A Reference Grammar*, Vol. 81. Italian Language. $28

ROSS TALARICO, *Sled Run*, Vol. 80. Fiction. $15

FRED MISURELLA, *Only Sons*, Vol. 79. Fiction. $14

FRANK LENTRICCHIA, *The Portable Lentricchia*, Vol. 78. Fiction. $16

RICHARD VETERE, *The Other Colors in a Snow Storm*, Vol. 77. Poetry. $10

GARIBALDI LAPOLLA, *Fire in the Flesh*, Vol. 76 Fiction & Criticism. $25

GEORGE GUIDA, *The Pope Stories*, Vol. 75 Prose. $15

ROBERT VISCUSI, *Ellis Island*, Vol. 74. Poetry. $28

ELENA GIANINI BELOTTI, *The Bitter Taste of Strangers Bread*, Vol. 73, Fiction, $24

PINO APRILE, *Terroni*, Vol. 72, Italian Studies, $20

EMANUEL DI PASQUALE, *Harvest*, Vol. 71, Poetry, $10

ROBERT ZWEIG, *Return to Naples*, Vol. 70, Memoir, $16

AIROS & CAPPELLI, *Guido*, Vol. 69, Italian/American Studies, $12

FRED GARDAPHÉ, *Moustache Pete is Dead! Long Live Moustache Pete!*, Vol. 67, Literature/Oral History, $12

PAOLO RUFFILLI, *Dark Room/Camera oscura*, Vol. 66, Poetry, $11

HELEN BAROLINI, *Crossing the Alps*, Vol. 65, Fiction, $14

COSMO FERRARA, *Profiles of Italian Americans*, Vol. 64, Italian Americana, $16

GIL FAGIANI, *Chianti in Connecticut*, Vol. 63, Poetry, $10

BASSETTI & D'ACQUINO, *Italic Lessons*, Vol. 62, Italian/American Studies, $10

CAVALIERI & PASCARELLI, Eds., *The Poet's Cookbook*, Vol. 61, Poetry/Recipes, $12

EMANUEL DI PASQUALE, *Siciliana*, Vol. 60, Poetry, $8

NATALIA COSTA, Ed., *Bufalini*, Vol. 59, Poetry. $18.

RICHARD VETERE, *Baroque*, Vol. 58, Fiction. $18.

LEWIS TURCO, *La Famiglia/The Family*, Vol. 57, Memoir, $15

NICK JAMES MILETI, *The Unscrupulous*, Vol. 56, Humanities, $20

BASSETTI, ACCOLLA, D'AQUINO, *Italici: An Encounter with Piero Bassetti*, Vol. 55, Italian Studies, $8

GIOSE RIMANELLI, *The Three-legged One*, Vol. 54, Fiction, $15

CHARLES KLOPP, *Bele Antiche Stòrie*, Vol. 53, Criticism, $25

JOSEPH RICAPITO, *Second Wave*, Vol. 52, Poetry, $12

GARY MORMINO, *Italians in Florida*, Vol. 51, History, $15

GIANFRANCO ANGELUCCI, *Federico F.*, Vol. 50, Fiction, $15

ANTHONY VALERIO, *The Little Sailor*, Vol. 49, Memoir, $9

ROSS TALARICO, *The Reptilian Interludes*, Vol. 48, Poetry, $15

RACHEL GUIDO DE VRIES, *Teeny Tiny Tino's Fishing Story*, Vol. 47, Children's Literature, $6

EMANUEL DI PASQUALE, *Writing Anew*, Vol. 46, Poetry, $15

MARIA FAMÀ, *Looking For Cover*, Vol. 45, Poetry, $12

ANTHONY VALERIO, *Toni Cade Bambara's One Sicilian Night*, Vol. 44, Poetry, $10

EMANUEL CARNEVALI, Dennis Barone, Ed., *Furnished Rooms*, Vol. 43, Poetry, $14

BRENT ADKINS, et al., Ed., *Shifting Borders, Negotiating Places*, Vol. 42, Proceedings, $18

GEORGE GUIDA, *Low Italian*, Vol. 41, Poetry, $11

GARDAPHÈ, GIORDANO, TAMBURRI, *Introducing Italian Americana*, Vol. 40, Italian/American Studies, $10

DANIELA GIOSEFFI, *Blood Autumn/Autunno di sangue*, Vol. 39, Poetry, $15/$25

www.ingramcontent.com/pod-product-compliance
Lightning Source LLC
Chambersburg PA
CBHW062055270326
41931CB00013B/3085